THE MOST FAMILIAR FACE
IN THE WORLD

GEORGE SKELLY

MAPLE
PUBLISHERS

The Most Familiar Face In the World

Author: George Skelly

Copyright © George Skelly (2021)

The right of George Skelly to be identified as author of this work has been asserted by the author in accordance with section 77 and 78 of the Copyright, Designs and Patents Act 1988 and/or any equivalent European and/or international law.

First published in 2021.

ISBN 978-1-914366-94-9 (Paperback)
978-1-914366-95-6 (Ebook)

Book layout by:
White Magic Studios
www.whitemagicstudios.co.uk

Cover design © George Skelly

Published by:
Maple Publishers
1 Brunel Way
Slough
SL1 1FQ
www.maplepublishers.com

For my dear friend, the late Lou Santangeli,
a noble fighter against injustice.

ABOUT THE AUTHOR

George Skelly, was educated at Ruskin College, Oxford and Liverpool University. He is the author of the acclaimed true crime books, *Murderers or Martyrs* and *The Cameo Conspiracy*. The latter helped to clear an innocent man's name of a 53 year-old murder. *The Most Familiar Face In The World* is his first novel. A father of four, he lives in Merseyside.

AUTHOR'S NOTE

This book had its genesis in the early 1970s, before being variously interrupted by the normal events of life: raising a family, voluntary work, higher education, a career in social work and years of campaigning and writing about miscarriages of justice.

The story, set in post-war Liverpool and seen through the eyes of the extraordinarily sensitive young Sheridan, is essentially about the inescapability of ourselves from ourselves, and the universal and timeless human need of having something to look forward to.

George Skelly, 2021.

Chapter One

Autumn 1946

He became really scared when he saw the gates being locked behind him and his Mam silently waving goodbye. What would it be like? That scared feeling was quickly becoming one of near hysteria now. But he knew, even at six years old, not to show any sign of this terrible fear. After all, what about all these others whose mams had also left them to flounder in this strange place? He didn't know and he didn't care. All he knew was that he felt all closed in and abandoned and sick with dread.

His big brothers, Brendan and Thomas, had both walked through these same gates years ago just like him. But before they'd finally left, they'd both been Cock of the Infants, then Cock of the Whole School. That's why he knew - although no one had said anything - that he too would be expected to fight his way to the same supreme position.

Shortly after all the mams had left, a stout middle-aged lady dressed in a grey tweed costume positioned herself outside the Infants' entrance at the top end of the schoolyard near to the main road. Whilst violently shaking a large wooden-handled bell with one hand, she began shuffling the kids into orderly columns of pairs.

He'd already become friendly with a smaller round-faced kid, who seemed just as scared as himself. This kid offered him a piece of cake his mam had packed for him to eat with his morning milk, which he greedily accepted, more the gesture than anything else, glad he wasn't alone in this strange frightening world. But before they had time to find out each other's names, a tall, thin, waxen-faced woman approached them.

"Come on you boys", she commanded sternly, "line up properly!"

With her thin lips and rimless glasses, she looked really cruel. And there was no sympathy or feeling in her voice, as she hustled them towards separate columns.

Instead of his new found friend, he was saddened to find himself paired with a small fair-haired girl with a shy grin. But luckily, the columns would not be the actual classes, because once inside the corridor they were sorted out and sent to their different classrooms. The round-faced kid was going to be in his class after all. And for the first time since arriving in this strange place, he felt a faint glimmer of relief. But the despondency soon returned when he discovered that, for some unknown reason, he was seated at the rear of the classroom far away from his friend in the front row.

When morning Playtime came, there were several boys and girls clinging to the schoolyard railings, which fronted onto the main road. All were crying for their mams and ignoring the efforts of various teachers trying to comfort them. But their cries and whimpering were drowned out by the occasional tramcar trundling past. He wished he too could cry like that and be comforted with attention from grown-ups, but instead turned to Roundface and, pretending to be brave, said, "Look at them little cissies crying to go home. It's alright here, isn't it?"

"Yeah" replied the other bravely. "I'm not scared, are you?"

"Naw, course not. There's nowt to be scared of is there?"

He then asked Roundface his name and how old he was because seniority, even of weeks, was very important at their age. His name was Winston Sanders, he said. And when he discovered his birthday was on the fourth of July, the same as his own, he was overjoyed and convinced that here he had a friend for life.

"That's a funny name though, isn't it?" he said. "Never heard of anyone being called Winston before. Is it German or something?"

"I don't know", he replied. "But me mam said it's a famous name. She said I've always got to be proud of it. Anyway", he went on, "what's yours?"

"Sheridan. Sheridan Connolly."

"Sheridan!" he exclaimed. "Never heard of a name like that."

"It's Irish, that's why", he replied. But quickly added, "*I'm* not Irish though."

After the name swapping, they began eating the two small apples Sheridan's Mam had given him and started playing Tick. But suddenly a bigger boy with a shock of unruly ginger hair, rushed head on at Sheridan and pushed him to the ground.

"What was that for?" he asked, wiping his grazed and dirtied kneecap.

The boy, whose face was almost covered in freckles, simply sneered at him challengingly without answering. But one of his friends, an under-nourished looking, but unusually well-clothed kid, boasted, "If you wanna play Tick, you've got to play it with us. No one else plays Tick only us." Then, nodding towards a smirking Freckles, he added, "He's the Cock of the Infants."

"Alright", he muttered. "I didn't know. Can we play in your game then?" This time Freckles himself answered. "If you wanna play with us, you'll have to bring me some cake or some apples tomorrow." Then to emphasise his threat, he slapped Winston across the face saying, "And *you too* big 'ead." They both agreed to pay the bribes but feeling sick at this evil of their strange new world, they lost all enthusiasm for any more games. Instead, they drifted over to the high railings and silently peered out longingly beyond the locked gates onto the busy main road, each hoping to be rescued from this alien place, but each ashamed to let the other see his fear.

When he arrived home at four o'clock, Sheridan didn't mention anything about this first frightening day at school. Too ashamed of himself, he knew the ridicule he would suffer from his Dad and brother Thomas for submitting to Freckles' threats. But he knew the apples of the first day were a rare luxury; he wouldn't be getting any more now till Duck-Apple Night. He knew that for sure because, although his Mam always said that Halloween wasn't Halloween without Duck-Apples, she could rarely afford them.

That night he slept fitfully at the foot of Thomas's bed. His brother, who was nearly sixteen would easily be able to fight Freckles, who couldn't be more than seven. But he quickly dismissed the thought. His shame and his pride wouldn't allow him to even dream of telling him. But the nervous heavy feeling in his belly kept him awake long after Thomas was snoring his head off.

One moment he thought about how easy it would be tomorrow if he just ignored Freckles. Just maybe he would leave him alone if he didn't make himself noticeable. He then thought of resisting him, but immediately dismissed that as too daunting.

This conflict raged within him long into the night, until he suddenly felt a surge of anger and determination. He knew that the only way was to face up to Freckles tomorrow and have it out with him. And once the bold decision had been made, he began to fall asleep - more from exhaustion than anything else.

When sleep finally came it was scarred with horrible nightmares. But there was one brief patch of relief as he dreamt he was beating the hell out of Freckles, with the packed schoolyard of kids witnessing his great triumph.

The next morning when his Mam shook him out of his "escape", Sheridan felt sick and miserable at the encounter that lay ahead. Freckles wouldn't be the Cock if he couldn't fight, would he? he thought. And he was bigger. And he really did look tough.

Trudging to school in the biting wind and rain, he shuddered. But as cold and bleak as the morning was, he knew that wasn't the reason. He'd thought about pretending to his Mam that he was sick, so that she would keep him off school, but immediately felt a faint disgust at himself. He'd also thought about pretending that he didn't know the way to school so that she would escort him, but quickly dropped the notion when he realised what that would mean. If he did get a good hiding off Freckles, the last thing he wanted was for his Mam to witness it, especially when he remembered her telling his Dad about how she'd seen Brendan challenging and beating the Cock of the Whole School in front of crowds of cheering lads. Bloody 'ell! he thought, why did Brendan and Thomas have to be such good fighters!

Once inside the schoolyard, Sheridan spotted Freckles leaning against the railings with several of his gang. Trying to be as inconspicuous as possible, he fixed his gaze on the ground and moved slowly back down the yard out of his sight. Maybe he wasn't really serious yesterday, he thought, and if he doesn't see me, he might forget all about it.

The barred gates at both ends of the schoolyard were now locked and the heavy feeling of dread assailed him with renewed force. Even the sight of friendly Winston approaching did nothing to lessen it.

"Hiya, Sheridan", he cheerfully cried. "Have yer got some cake or something for the Cock? I have." Feeling betrayed and alone, he watched with dismay as Winston pulled out a brown paper bag from his jacket pocket. With a dejected expression, he replied, "No, me Mam didn't give me anything this morning."

"Well, it's alright", said Winston, "I've brought some cake and jam butties, so's he won't hit us."

As they spoke, Freckles and his gang were slowly approaching. Sheridan felt his mouth suddenly go dry and the heavy feeling of dread in his belly returning. Trying not to notice, he panicked inside and began talking to Winston quickly and tastelessly in the hope of somehow shutting out the menace that was almost upon him.

With his gang making a circle around the two small figures, Freckles asked Winston, "What have yer brought us then?"

"Here yer are", he confidently replied as he handed him the small parcel. As the smug-faced others looked on, proud to be mates of the Cock, one of them mischievously elbowed Sheridan in the stomach. Seeing this, Freckles immediately turned on him. "Leave him for a minute", he commanded. Opening the parcel of a jam butty and two cupcakes, he concentrated on Winston.

"Listen you, big 'ead", he ordered, "tomorrow I want some sherbert and toffee, or you've had it. D'yer hear?" Looking downcast at this further demand, Winston silently nodded his agreement, even though he knew the toffee would be impossible because of the sweet rationing.

Before Freckles could demand anything from Sheridan, he told him he was sorry he'd forgotten to bring some apples, but that he would bring some the next day.

In addition to feeling disgusted with himself for having to lie like this, he also felt desperately frightened, because he knew he would not be able to bring any apples tomorrow either. He knew he was merely postponing his fate. Yet, in order to stave off an attack, he perversely added a further inducement. "Think me Mam'll give me threepence tomorrow as well", he pleaded. "I'll ask her anyway." But Freckles would have none of it. Grabbing him by his jersey collar, he hissed through gritted teeth, "I told yer to bring me something today, didn't I? Well, where is it?" Unable to think of anything more to say, Sheridan could only timidly whisper, "I've already told yer." Maintaining his grip on his collar, Freckles began to lightly slap his face back and forth whilst muttering chastisingly in a staccato rhythm, "I - told - yer - to - bring - me - something - didn't - I." This caused the others to start laughing, because Freckles was so funny when he carried on like this.

At first the slaps, back and forth with the palm and the back of his hand, didn't really hurt Sheridan. The repetitive scorn and humiliation hurt more. But gradually the cumulative effect of the slaps began to smart, and his face actually began to redden. But still it wasn't a serious pain, more of a nuisance pain. What hurt him more than anything else - much more than if a grown-up or his Dad was doing it - was that it was a boy like himself doing it to him.

Under the constant slapping, Sheridan's eyes were now watering, and his face felt on fire. The surrounding sea of faces, no matter where they positioned themselves, were all deeply focused on him - penetrating, mocking, derisory, hateful and laughing. And ringing in his ears, in time with the slaps, was the hideous falsetto voice of his tormentor repeating over and over again, "What - are - yer - gonna - bring - me? What - are - yer - gonna - bring - me?" Yet for some reason he couldn't hear his own muted, but equally repetitive, concession, "Some apples and money, apples and money..."

Somewhere in the mocking mass of enemy faces, he suddenly caught a glance of friendly Winston's. At least, he thought, everything's not bad. There's one friend. But this fleeting reassurance quickly evaporated as he saw Winston begin to smile. At first the smile was begrudging, but as he felt himself drawn more and more into the herd of camaraderie, it blossomed into outright amusement then into full blown laughter. This hit him with a terrible impact and left him feeling totally betrayed. Then, deep inside himself, he felt a desperate rumbling lava of tears, which suddenly erupted and spilled out in torrents down his burning face. And with them came an almighty stream of uncontrollable intolerance. He'd had enough of this strange hostile hand slapping him across the face. It seemed as if it was going to last forever! Wasn't it ever going to stop? And the other hand at his throat? It was nearly choking him! What was it doing there anyway? And that face! That close-up face, which was mesmerising him; that landscape of ugly red spots; those uneven broken teeth, as the thin snarling mouth opened and closed like a gnawing rat's; the spittle, which was now sporadically hitting his face? It was all so hateful. So alien.

The lava of anger soon followed, as he suddenly kicked out at his tormentor. But as he did so, he immediately felt a new, different kind of pain, much worse than the slaps, as Freckles punched him hard in the face. At this, he lost all self-control, as he felt himself hitting out with tightly clenched fists, straight and regular like an engine's pistons, just like his Dad had shown him. Unaware of who or where or what his target was, he was now overcome by sheer blind fury.

Freckles, who had been forced to release his grip on Sheridan's collar, now adopted a sparring pose. This stance was for the benefit of his admiring audience, but he also hoped it would sufficiently impress this wild thing to call off his attack. But it didn't work, for he suddenly felt his shins scorching with pain as Sheridan's boots lashed out at him. Then, before he knew it, this mad unmanageable thing was close-up, hurting him, pounding away at his face, his arms, his body, with hard ramrod fists. Despite this, he desperately tried to hang on, but the assault proved too overwhelming, as he finally sank to the ground.

By now the crowd had grown until practically the whole of the Infants were witnessing the battle; those at the rear jumping on the backs of the lucky ringsiders and the ringsiders creating an infectious animal atmosphere as they encouraged everyone to join them in their chanting of, "Hoo! Hoo! Hoo! Hoo!"

The two fighters were now wrestling furiously on the playground's hard gravel surface. And even though he was underneath, Freckles managed once more to get a tight grip on Sheridan's jersey collar. Feeling that he was slowly being choked to death, he then insanely began to pummel the freckled face of the Cock with both fists.

The entire situation was so unreal to him. It was as if he were in one of those horrible nightmares of last night. But strangely, unlike in the nightmares, he wasn't afraid anymore. All he was certain of was that he must destroy this hateful object, who was making his life so unbearably miserable.

"Yer bastard! Yer bastard!" he cursed with each punch, as he sensed Freckles - who had released his grip in order to protect his face - was slowly fading. Keeping up the relentless maniacal assault, he continued to pound away at Freckles' face. It was now involuntary. A victim of his own blind fury, he was now fighting on pure instinct. All he knew was to keep punching, keep hitting, keep hurting.

Powerful hands finally grabbed Sheridan under the arms and dragged him away. The "Hoo, hoo, hoo", of the infant spectators gradually faded away, to be replaced by silence and frightened looks. Freckles, curled up on the ground like a hedgehog, was howling in pain. Two female teachers then hustled Sheridan through the silent throng towards the Infants' entrance.

On the way he heard a very nice-looking dark-haired girl admiringly say to someone, "Wow'er, he can't half fight, can't he?" The way she said it made him feel great. He didn't know if this fight with Freckles would change anything, but at least, he thought, it can't go back to being any worse.

Now in the Headmistress's study, he was flanked by the plump bell-ringer and Waxen Face of yesterday. The grey-haired Headmistress, Mrs Dodson, tidily dressed in her brown costume and cream blouse, had a kindly face, but her manner was not kindly. "This is disgraceful boy", she angrily chided. "We simply cannot have children like you fighting and swearing in the school playground."

He didn't remember seeing her in the playground, but he guessed it must have been Waxen Face, rather than the other teacher, who had told her all about the fight.

Waxen Face didn't seem to like him, he thought, from the first moment she'd set eyes on him. There was a certain look she'd given him when she'd partnered him with the little shy girl yesterday: a snooty look which seemed to sneeringly say, "I don't care how good or how clever or how well-behaved you pretend to be, you won't fool me, because I know what kind of a scruffy person you are, and from what a drunken scruffy home you come from." And this disheartened him, because he wasn't trying to fool anybody.

When Waxen Face told Mrs Dodson of how he had "frenziedly" attacked the other boy and kicked and swore at him, he guessed his suspicions about her had been right. Suddenly, he didn't feel the need to tell his side of it. It seemed hopeless anyway, because they all sounded as if they'd already made up their minds about who was to blame.

"You are a very naughty boy", continued Mrs Dodson, sounding even angrier. "We just cannot have this sort of behaviour in our school!" Waxen Face looked smug, the other teacher sympathetic, as she went on, "Now before we do anything else, you can go and wash your grubby little face. You look disgraceful." Then addressing Waxen Face, she asked, "Does he know how to wash himself, Miss Jones?" But before she could answer, Sheridan butted in. "I've been able to wash myself since I was four, miss", he said, proud of the mild defiance in his tone. "Right then", said the Headmistress, "go to the washbasins and get a thorough wash, and don't forget your neck and behind your ears. Then come right back here. Do you understand?"

"Yes, miss", he respectfully replied.

Returning some minutes later, his face, although still scarlet from the exertion and anxiety of the fight, was unmarked and scrupulously clean.

A door in the Headmistress's study led to a small toilet where there was also a washbasin. Leading him inside, whilst still lecturing him about his disgraceful behaviour, she said in a softer tone, "Now, what I'm going to do... you know those dreadful swear words you came out with? Well, we shall have to completely remove them. If we don't, they will always be there and you will probably start swearing again. So, we'll have to make sure we get rid of them once and for all, won't we?" Fascinated watching her prepare a small nailbrush in warm water and lather it with the colourless bar of carbolic soap, he made no reply.

"Now, open wide", she commanded, "and put your tongue right out."

Feeling silly, but awed in the face of such authority, he did as he was told.

"We've really got to make sure all those nasty words are wiped away forever, haven't we?" she muttered kindly as she scrubbed across his tongue with the hard bristled brush.

When she had finished, she told him to go back to the washbasins and give his mouth a good rinsing out. But before he could reach them, he made the mistake of swallowing, which caused him to vomit violently. To make matters worse, as he shamefacedly looked around, he saw Waxen Face standing over him. With a look of disgust and contempt, she quietly said, "You dirty, filthy, little boy." Then raising her voice, she ordered, "Well, go on then, get the mop and clear this mess up!"

He gave his mouth a refreshing rinse with cold water and got rid of the sickening carbolic taste. But try as he may, he could not manage the mop, it was too big and too heavy. But thankfully, a passing teacher helpfully finished the task for him.

Returning to rejoin his class, he began thinking about how the Headmistress had said you could actually wash swear words off your tongue forever. He'd never heard of that before. He thought it was stupid. But school *was* a strange, funny place. What if she was right? He couldn't resist giving it a try... just to see. So, walking down the empty corridor, he whispered to himself, "Bastard." Surprised to find the word still on his tongue, he reasoned that perhaps it was only the really bad ones which were rubbed off forever. So before reaching the classroom, he again whispered with stolen devilment, "fuck, fucker, cunt, twat, slut, whore." As he suspected, they were all still there. He knew they would be. His Mam and Dad had been saying them since he could remember. Planting a lasting disrespect deep inside himself for the Headmistress, he thought, "She must think I'm fuckin' stupid!"

When he entered the classroom, everybody suddenly became quiet, the other children nudging each other and staring at him. He was the centre of attention, with the girls doing most of the staring and nudging. Observing this, their teacher, Miss Campbell, a tall, wiry, bespectacled woman, climbed down from her high Dickensian desk and brought him to the front of the class.

"Now children", she began demonstrably as if he were an exhibit in a lesson, "Sheridan Connolly here has been very naughty this morning. He has been fighting and swearing in the playground and..."

"Yes, miss. We saw him, miss", chorused the whole class in condemnation. "Quiet now children. That is the first thing we must learn", she continued. "We must not interrupt when others are talking. Nor will we have bad behaviour anywhere in school. It's a shocking thing", she went on, "to have used the terrible bad language this boy used. So he will have to be punished, and this goes for all of you if you behave as badly as he has done."

Sheridan didn't feel altogether ashamed, part of him felt quite proud, but he was curious about what his latest punishment was going to be. He did not have to wait long, as Miss Campbell then told the class, "He will go and stand outside in the corridor for the rest of the morning. He will not be allowed out for Playtime, and none of you are to speak to him. And when he realises what a very bad boy he has been, he will be allowed to come back into class this afternoon." Then, addressing him for the first time, she said, "Now off you go outside. And don't forget, no Playtime for you." Feeling much more ashamed than when he had entered a few minutes earlier, he slunk ignominiously out of the classroom.

Afterwards, when the whole of the Infants piled out for Playtime, he was left standing alone in the empty corridor. So with nothing else to do, he began repeating the swear words, and this gave him a great feeling of defiance and satisfaction. Earlier, as everyone was leaving, he had spotted Freckles among them. His face was red and lumpy and his left eye looked swollen. And although he had seen Sheridan, he had quickly lowered his gaze, avoiding looking him in the face. But this told him nothing: he still didn't know whether Freckles was still mad at him or ashamed of himself.

Now in the deserted corridor, he saw a lone figure approaching. Unable to make out his features, he somehow sensed it was Freckles. "Hiya", he whispered. "Here's a piece of rhubarb pie for yer. Your mate, Winston, told me you'd been kept in." Sheridan was lost for words. His first thought was that Freckles was coming to get his revenge. He was actually getting ready to say sorry, because he didn't want another fight. Even now he couldn't believe he'd actually stood up to the Cock! He could never have planned such a challenge. He knew it was his rage rather than cold courage which had won his battle. But seeing how respectful Freckles now was, he quickly concealed his surprise and fear and tried to act assured. "Ta", he said. Then mindful of his own punishment he asked, "What happened to you?"

"Nothing", he replied. "They didn't touch me. They only took you to Mrs Dodson because you won. When yer win the fight, they always take yer to her room."

Suddenly, he felt deliriously happy. Freckles' admission that he'd beaten him had removed the biggest threat to his happiness in this unhappy place. He felt so grateful and immediately wanted to make friends with him. But before he could do so, Freckles offered his little finger and said, "Shall we make friends, eh? Cos I've gotta go now. We're not supposed to be in here of a Playtime." As Sheridan eagerly locked his little finger in his and "shook" on it, Freckles, running back down the corridor shouted back, "I'll see yer at dinner time, eh?"

"Yeah, okay", he called after him as he began tucking into the piece of rhubarb pie and feeling truly happy for the first time in his short life.

Chapter Two

1950

Sheridan's eldest brother, Brendan, was a private in the King's Regiment. He had been stationed in the Canal Zone in the Middle East for about three months now. And since he'd gone away, life at home had become much more unhappy.

When Brendan was home on leave, it was nice. Sheridan always felt warm and safe. When his Dad came in drunk of a night - which he usually did - there was less chance of him beating up his Mam and smashing up the house if Brendan was there, because he always jumped in and stopped it. And he was really kind to him too. He never shouted at him or hit him like Thomas did. And when he'd go on errands for him, even if only for five Woodbines, he would always give him a threepenny bit or a sixpence. And he always asked nicely if he wanted him to do anything. He never forced him like Thomas did.

When their Mam and Dad were out in the pub every Friday night, Thomas always made him stay in to black-lead the fire grate and scrub the hearth and do a thousand other tasks. But Brendan, when he was home, would give him tenpence to go to the "Hopey" picture house. And God help Thomas if he tried to hit him or order him around when Brendan was there. He'd kill him!

Another thing he loved about Brendan was his army uniform, and the smell of the Brasso, which he polished his brasses and buttons with, and the Blanco he used for his white gaiters and belt and lanyard. He would sit for hours just watching Brendan polishing his shiny black boots, one little finger stuck inside the orange polishing rag, spitting like a snake and making millions of little circles around the toecaps until you could even see your face in them. He'd spend hours pressing his uniform with the old flat iron and polishing and Brasso-ing. And when he went out looking really smart, Sheridan would feel so proud of his big brother. He must have been the smartest soldier in the whole British Army, he thought.

But Brendan wasn't here now, as Thomas, lounging in the armchair, commanded scornfully, "Hey dogsbody, come here!"

It was Friday night and their Mam and Dad were out drinking, as usual.

As long as he could remember, Sheridan had never known his Dad to be sober on a Friday or Saturday night. He couldn't even imagine his Dad being sober at weekends. It would feel so strange, he thought, like finding a Martian or something in the house.

Other kids at school often told him how their dads took them to the pictures on a Friday night or, on Saturday afternoons, to the footy match at Anfield or Goodison Park, or shopping downtown, or took them fishing. But his Dad never did anything like that. He was too busy drinking. That, and the fighting with his Mam, was so regular, it was normal. He'd never known things to be otherwise. To see his Dad sober, sitting in the old armchair by the fire on a Friday or Saturday night would have been the most wonderful thing in the world, he often thought. But then again, it would have seemed so unreal.

Instead, it was Thomas who was now slouched in this raggedy chair, which had once been the pride of some well-off Victorian family, his legs lazily straddled across the threadbare bulky arm as he skimmed through a *Captain Marvel* comic. He always acted like this when they were alone - like some power-crazed ruler.

Standing obediently before him full of trepidation, Sheridan meekly asked, "What d'yer want?"

"Go down and get me a bowl of water", he ordered, "and fill the kettle while you're at it."

This command terrified him, for the tap was in the cellar and there was no light down there. And, if there was one thing he was scared of, it was the dark.

"Ah eh, kid", he begged, "Yer know I'm scared. It's pitch black down there."

"Don't be fuckin' soft", said Thomas. "Yer can take the candle, can't yer?"

"It's not only the dark though", he moaned. "What about the slugs? There's millions of them down there."

Brushing aside his plea with a contempt that reminded Sheridan of Freckles on that first day at school, he hissed menacingly, "I said go 'an get a bowl of water, didn't I? Now get a fuckin' move on, yer lazy little cunt."

Despite his fear, he realised there was no way out of this. Thomas was going with his mates to the *Palais-de-Luxe* tonight to see John Wayne in *Red River*. He needed a kettle-full of water to heat, in order to get a wash.

At one time, when he went to the Hopey, like the rest of the kids in the street, Thomas sometimes never even bothered to get a wash. But since he'd left school, he hardly ever went there now, and always had to have a wash before going out.

The Hopey, whose real name was the *Hope Hall* after the Evangelist chapel it once was, was only a few streets away, but it was a "bug-house". People in the cushioned seats in the one-and-sixes were always complaining of itching and finding bugs on themselves when they left. And the films they showed were years old.

Thomas seemed proud of the fact that he no longer had to stand outside that fleapit asking grown-ups to take him in because he wasn't old enough to be admitted on his own. In any case, even though he was now old enough to take himself in, he wouldn't be found dead in the Hopey these days. He still went regularly to the pictures, but now it was to proper cinemas like the *Majestic* or the *Forum* or the *Futurist* or the *Scala*, or the *Palais-de-Luxe* downtown on Lime Street.

Not wishing to upset Thomas any further, Sheridan reluctantly looped his right arm under the handle of the grimy kettle, then with both hands gripped the sides of the huge enamel bowl, full of dirty dishwater.

"Light the candle for us then", he asked as the kettle swung freely on his arm.

Lighting a half-used, misshapen candle from the mantelpiece, Thomas muttered, "There, yer stupid little bastard."

Looking anxious, Sheridan began making his way down the dark, creaky stairs. But trying, as he was, to grip both the bowl and candle, this caused the hot wax to drip onto the back of his hand. It burned at first, but he endured the pain, as he tried to reach the cellar as quickly as possible without tripping over or spilling any water.

The hot wax reminded him of the first time he'd had it on his skin. It must have been about three years ago, he thought. Anyway, it was long before Thomas had left school.

That night he and Thomas, as usual, had taken the candle upstairs to see themselves to bed because, the only source of lighting was a gas mantle and that was in the living room. When they were both in bed, they couldn't sleep so Thomas started telling him stories of the films he'd seen on the Hopey.

Thomas was crazy about films. He'd seen hundreds of them - mostly about cowboys or soldiers. And it was always John Wayne who was the hero of the stories. He was mad about John Wayne. But Sheridan thought he must have made up the stories half the time, because John Wayne couldn't have been in all of those pictures without ever being killed - even once.

That first night of the hot candle wax, Thomas hadn't been to the Hopey for two weeks and had no more stories... or so he said. So to relieve the boredom, he reached for the lighted candle perched on top of the brass bed post of their old iron bed.

"D'yer want me to show yer how to make chewy?" he asked.

Before Sheridan could reply, he had the candle tilted over the back of his own outstretched hand with the hot wax falling in steady droplets. In no time it was covered in a thick film of candle grease. Then after it had cooled and become a little solid, he began to peel it off with his teeth, chewing it around in his mouth until finally spitting it out in a ball into the palm of his hand.

"There yer are", he said proudly, "real Yankee chewing gum. Come on now, give us *your* hand."

It really hurt at first, but Thomas told him to stop crying and acting like a little cissy, as he grabbed hold of his wrist and slowly dripped the burning wax onto the back of his hand until it was completely covered. Scraping it off with his teeth, he thought it didn't taste all that bad, but as soon as Thomas fell asleep, he spat it out into the fireplace.

They'd done it many times since that night. But around the time he left school, Thomas stopped doing it. That's when he started going to the posh picture houses too. He never told stories anymore either. Sheridan had to stop too, because nowadays when they were in bed, Thomas was always telling him to blow the candle out and stop messing around.

Before they'd stopped, he had got so used to the burning that he hardly felt it. And the pain was a small price to pay for being able to make your own chewy, because with the sweet rationing you hardly ever saw any *real* chewing gum.

Now, as he warily descended the stairs, the wax was dripping remorselessly, and because he hadn't done it for a long time it was really hurting him. It seemed to burn more than it had ever done, and he was glad when he finally reached the sanctuary of the old stone sink in the far corner of the cellar.

After letting a few drops of wax drip onto the edge of the chipped brown sink, he fixed the upright candle in its soft foundation so it wouldn't fall off. And because it was so cold down here it set almost immediately. He then delicately emptied the bowl of dirty, greasy water, careful not to splash the candle in case it went out.

He knew they were there. They always were. But no matter how many times he saw them, they still sent a cold shiver through him. Now here they were again: the sickening, slimy green and yellow slugs, creeping out of the rotten, damp wall and curling themselves around the old lead pipe. Verging on panic, he tried to avert his gaze, looking around anywhere and everywhere but at the infested pipe and tap, until the bowl and kettle were filled.

When he finally got back upstairs, Thomas thumped him across the back of his neck, because he had spilled most of the water and hadn't cleaned the dirty grease off the inside of the bowl. The slugs had been too terrifying for him to waste time removing that!

As he started crying, Thomas again turned on him.

"Yer can cut that out right away", he shouted, "or I'll give yer something to cry for!"

Then, placing the kettle on the gas stove, he continued relentlessly, "When I come in tonight, I want to see this place tidied up and all these dishes washed. D'yer hear me?"

Sheridan nodded in between sobs, knowing that this would mean another journey down to the cellar and the slugs.

I wish this bastard would get run over by a truck or something, he thought. I hate him! I hate him! Do me best to keep in with him, but he still keeps picking on me and hitting me. I hate the fuckin' bastard!

He would never ever like him the way he liked Brendan, he thought. He really *loved* Brendan. And the warm memories of his protector so far across the seas, made him sob so heavily he could hardly catch his breath.

But there was no respite from Thomas. "If yer don't fuckin' well shut up, yer stupid bleeder, you'll go to fuckin' bed right now!" he roared.

Although feeling powerless against this far superior force, he still couldn't stop crying. And Thomas was now beginning to really lose his temper. "Right!" he exclaimed, "I'll count to three for yer to shut up!" But the despair was involuntary now: the sobs and tears could not be stemmed. "One", cried Thomas. Then after a brief pause, "Two!" He realised Sheridan wasn't going to stop, but he daren't lose face now.

"Are yer going to stop?" he demanded, giving him one last chance. But Sheridan's sobbing was now out of control.

"Three!"

Lunging at him suddenly, Thomas threw him over his shoulder. "Right, yer cheeky little bastard", he cried, "think yer can fuckin' defy me do yer! You're going to fuckin' bed right now!" At this hostile action, Sheridan felt his breathing getting even shorter. Why was this hatred directed at him? What had he done? As the injustice of the situation beat down on him with a venom, he screamed out, more in despair than anger or defiance.

He had nothing to lose now, as he roared madly at Thomas carrying him roughly up the stairs. The bastard knew how much he was scared of the dark, he thought, yet here he was forcing him up to bed with no light. He no longer cared what he did to him now, because whatever he did couldn't be any worse than the dark.

"You fuckin' bastard!" he screamed hysterically. "You bastard! You bastard!"

In the darkness, Thomas threw him down violently onto the unmade bed. Sheridan's mad temper had caught him by surprise. So, not wanting to commit himself to a final and complete victory, he got out of the room before it turned into a major battle of wills. Besides, he couldn't be messed around any longer by this rebellious little bleeder. John Wayne was on the *Palais-de-Luxe* and he wasn't going to miss *him* for anyone, least of all this cheeky little bastard.

Descending the stairs, he could still hear Sheridan sobbing and making feeble threats between the sobs.

"Wait till me Mam comes in, that's all. Just you wait... just you wait!"

Defiant little bastard, he thought, slamming the kitchen door closed.

Sheridan sensed that his threats had been futile and hadn't bothered Thomas in the least. But if Brendan was home, he thought longingly, that would be a different matter. He wouldn't dare treat him like this if Brendan was here.

"Think yer big don't yer, 'cause no one's home", he cried out again, but doubting whether Thomas could even hear him. Nevertheless, he was glad to get this out and out defiance across.

"Just wait till Brenny comes home... just you wait... I'll tell him... I won't forget... he'll batter yer."

But, as he'd expected, there was only silence from downstairs.

The first tears had dried by now, making his eyes smart, and his nose feel all blocked up. But as a fresh wave of misery hit him, it was pleasing in a funny sort of way to feel the salty soreness in his eyes being soothed by the new tears cascading down his face. Burying his head in the lumpy flock pillow, his body shook as he beat his fists madly.

It was a long time before he finally stopped crying.

He didn't remember falling asleep, but he guessed he must have done so because he was suddenly awakened by his Dad's voice growing louder and louder as he sang his way down the street. He knew it must now be after ten o'clock, because his Dad never came home until the pubs closed.

He always felt a sense of dread inside when he'd hear his Dad singing on his way home from the pub. He'd get so miserable and scared that he'd always say a quick prayer. "Please God, don't let him start fighting with me Mam again." But he suspected that God couldn't be all that he was made out to be, because they usually ended up fighting anyway.

His ears had become so attuned to listening for his Dad, that he could more or less tell by the loudness of his singing, exactly how far away he was. When he'd first pick up the faint sound he would be somewhere near the corner of the street. Then when the volume was about medium, he would be halfway down the street. And when it became really loud, so that it sometimes made him tremble, he would be outside the front door. But even when there was no singing, he would still know when his Dad was outside by his shouting and banging on the front door, because the lock had been broken for ages and there was only a bolt on the inside.

The sound of his Dad was so embedded in him, that some nights, even a Sunday when he would be sober reading a newspaper downstairs, he would imagine he could still hear his raucous singing. But at those times, for some reason, it always seemed to stay at the same distant pitch and never got any louder.

Dragging himself off the unkempt bed in the dark, he quickly rubbed his eyes with his jersey sleeve in case anyone suspected he'd been crying. By now his Dad had temporarily stopped singing and was banging on the door shouting, "Aye! Aye! Open up will yer!"

Once again, he felt the surge of anxiety and dread. It always frightened him, this shouting. Why, he thought, couldn't he just whistle through the letterbox like Brendan and Thomas did? It seemed daft that his Dad couldn't do something that even hateful, stupid Thomas could do.

After hastily feeling his way to the top of the stairs, he was then able to make quicker progress because the kitchen door was ajar. And, guided down the stairs by the gaslight coming from the kitchen, he frantically raced along the lobby crying, "Alright! Alright! I'm coming."

Once inside the kitchen, his Dad immediately started singing again and pulled two quart bottles of ale out of his pockets. His Mam followed behind him and Sheridan noted, with a feeling of renewed dread, that she looked really drunk. The front door was banging to and fro because she had left it open, so he again dashed down the lobby to close it.

Back in the kitchen his Mam was pulling smaller bottles of beer out of her shopping bag with labels on them saying, "Nut Brown Ale" and "Guinness". Mumbling to herself, she put the bottles on the table and almost fell into the old armchair. Then, with a haughty look, she leaned her head backwards and looked his Dad up and down, as if disgusted by him. Sheridan hoped and prayed she wasn't going to start a fight. And for good luck, he crossed his fingers behind his back. His Dad also looked drunk. But *he* also looked happy. Sheridan was glad he hadn't seen the nasty look on his Mam's face.

It often seemed to Sheridan that there were two Dads, because he was like a different person when he was drunk. When he was sober, he always looked thin and his skin was pale, and he was always quiet and miserable. But when he was drunk, he was altogether different. His face became reddened and he seemed to be fatter and healthier and happier, and he was always smiling and talking and singing. The only thing that spoiled it was the fighting.

Standing, like he always did with his back to the fireplace, his Dad was singing now. The fire itself had long gone out, but he didn't seem to notice so long as he could sing. Suddenly, he stopped in mid-song and said, "Get some cups son and give yer mother a drink."

Then tapping his Mam on the shoulder, he asked, "Happy, Kate girl? Happy, girl?"

His Mam, her eyes now half-closed and her head sagging on her chest, didn't reply. But that didn't stop him from prodding her again and repeating the question. When he was drunk, he was always asking them all if they were happy.

Whilst his Dad began singing again, Sheridan quickly grabbed two chipped cups and asked which ale he should pour out. This time his Dad, now singing *Mammy*, finished the song before saying, "Go on lad, give yer mother a drink. Don't worry about me... I'm chocker... I've had a bellyful."

Pouring out two liberal cupfuls from the quart bottle, Sheridan placed his Mam's cup precariously on the soft bulky arm of the chair, as he tried to awaken her. But, without raising her sagging head, she simply mumbled something. He was glad she was asleep because, although his Dad would let him drink ale, she never would. And, even better, because she was so sleepy, it was now almost guaranteed there would be no fighting tonight!

As if reading his thoughts, his Dad invited him to drink the cupful of ale he'd poured for his Mam.

"She's had enough, she's bevvied", he said, "Had a bellyful, like me."

At first he pretended he didn't want any, but his Dad persisted.

"Go on, have a drop", he said. "Won't do yer any harm. Good laxative, mild beer."

Pleased and more relaxed now at the happy atmosphere, Sheridan took the cup from the arm of the chair and said, "Aw thanks, Dad."

The first mouthful tasted bitter, as it always did, and it made him shudder slightly, but as usual he quickly grew to like the taste. Slyly pretending it was for his Mam, he was soon pouring another cupful.

With his Dad absorbed in his singing and his Mam asleep in the chair, Sheridan helped himself to a few more cupfuls. Pretty soon he was imagining himself as a grown-up and pretending to be drunk. And when his Dad began singing *Ragtime Cowboy Joe*, with the big smile he always wore when he was drunk and happy, he was enjoying it so much he felt like joining in.

His Dad was a real good singer when he wanted to be, he thought, and was always singing Al Jolson songs. Sometimes he thought his Dad must have been as mad about Al Jolson as Thomas was about John Wayne.

Eventually, he sat down in the other decrepit armchair and began to sing *Sonny Boy*, a song which always made Sheridan sad. His Dad always sang this song really nice, he thought. He never sang it loud like most of the other songs, and he always looked real sad himself. It always made him feel like crying, and he suspected that his Dad felt like crying too when he was singing it, but he never did.

He knew that a long time ago, before he was born, he'd had a brother named Danny who had died when he was four. And whenever his Dad sang *Sonny Boy*, he'd always interrupt himself and say to his Mam, "Young Danny, Kate... poor little Danny", as if to remind her.

If he were alive today, he'd be older than Brendan. It would have been great, he thought, to have had another big brother like Brendan. But it would have also felt really strange in another way, because there could only ever be one Brendan.

Rising from the chair, his Dad now picked him up and hugged him as he continued to sing. This made him feel silly. It always did. And not only did the loudness of his voice, so close-up, make his ear tickle inside, but he hugged him so hard it nearly took his breath away. His Dad's face was so close, he could see his teeth, stained with years of drinking and smoking, with wide gaps between each one. But really, he loved the smell of his Dad; the smell of ale and tobacco. It was a real grown-up smell. But what he didn't like was what he was doing now: pulling him even closer and rubbing his unshaven face against his cheek. The stubble felt like sandpaper, scratching his face, making it all red and blotchy. But he knew his Dad didn't mean to hurt him. It was his way, when he was drunk, of showing how much he loved him... but it didn't half hurt.

"The angels were lonely, they took you and left me only, now I'm lonely too... Sonnee Boy."

The big broad smile had collapsed now as his Dad finally put him down.

Although the tears were unshed, Sheridan could see them in his Dad's eyes. But slowly rubbing his coat sleeve across his nose, he sniffed like a boxer trying to get more breath and the tears stayed inside

"Ah, well", he sighed to himself, "it's nice to be nice."

Then tapping his Mam's shoulder, he said a little louder, "Isn't that right, Kate? It's nice to be nice, isn't it girl?"

Getting no response, he gazed at the floor with a frown. But it was more a frown of sadness than bad temper. Then, emerging from his brief reverie with a dismissing swipe of his hand, he sighed, "Ah well! Close up those records fraught with such pain, for years that have vanished return not again."

All of the joy seemed to have left him. He suddenly seemed to be tired of everything. Sheridan didn't know why he'd started talking like this, but he knew it was from a poem he'd often heard him reciting. That was another good thing his Dad was good at, he thought - poetry. He knew hundreds of poems. He'd even learned one from him and had come top of the class for reciting it.

That was only a few months ago, just after he'd moved up to Junior 2. They'd all been told to memorise a piece of poetry out of the school textbook. But there wasn't much choice really, only *Daffodils* and *Young Ethelred*, and another about fairies at the bottom of the garden or something like that. But he thought they were too posh and cissy. He couldn't imagine himself standing in front of the class reciting any of those. Besides, his classmates were all learning one or other of these. So he thought that if he recited a poem that nobody knew, he would stand a better chance of coming top.

His Dad hadn't purposely taught him the poem. It was just that he'd heard him reciting it so often, every time he was drunk, that he knew it off by heart. He didn't even know what it was called, or who had written it. But he liked it, because his Dad had told him it was about an old man who had once been rich, but had ended up dying in the Workhouse. It reminded him of *Buddy Can You Spare A Dime*, one of the songs his Dad always sang.

When it was his turn, the teacher, Mr Henry, had told him to come and stand in front of the class. He felt nervous in case he forgot some of the words but decided to go in head first. But he only got as far as the opening line, *"Time has stolen all my youth...",* when, despite him being Cock of the Class, some of the kids at the back of the class started tittering. Mr Henry got really mad at them that day and threatened that, if there was any more laughter, Playtime would be stopped for a week. Then, giving Sheridan a sympathetic look, he said, "Go on Connolly, carry on."

Feeling awkward and nervous, he tried to get it over with as quickly as possible as he continued:

"...gone is all my gold.
Now I've learned Life's bitter truth
I am poor and old.
Time may dim my vision and leave me sad and grey,
But Life's enduring memories they cannot take away.
For deep in our breasts
what fond memories rest,
of the scenes and the places we knew.
The laughter and tears
that live through the years,
Dear pals who were loyal and true.
In moments of bliss
the sweet voice we miss,
whose echo still haunts us today.
What visions we hold
when Time makes us old,
Those memories they can't take away."

Feeling a mixture of embarrassment and shame, and glad the ordeal was finally over, he quickly returned to his desk.

With his face burning as he desperately fought to control the blushing, he could feel Mr Henry staring at him, which just made it worse. The silence in the classroom was deafening. You could have heard a pin drop, as Mr Henry continued staring at him for what seemed like ages, before finally ordering Winston Sanders to the front of the class.

As Winston stumbled through *Young Ethelred*, occasionally forgetting the next word or line, Sheridan began to feel more relaxed because Mr Henry had now stopped staring at him.

Later when everybody was leaving for Playtime, Mr Henry asked him to stay behind. He guessed why. He was probably going to be punished for reciting his own poem instead of one from the textbook. But, to his amazement and relief, the teacher, far from chastising him, said he thought it was an excellent poem and asked him its title.

"I don't know, sir", he truthfully replied.

"Well, where did you learn it then?" he asked coaxingly.

He hadn't learned it, he replied, he'd just automatically remembered it through his Dad always reciting it. But he never told him it was only when his Dad was drunk.

"What does your father do then, Connolly?"

He was now beginning to resent Mr Nosey-Parker Henry. What his Dad worked at was none of his business. But really, he knew it was more shame anything else, because his Dad hadn't had a job for years.

It wasn't the first time he'd been ashamed of his Dad not working. It was for the same reason that he'd told all his pals his Dad was a train driver. But somehow, he thought Mr Henry wouldn't swallow that lie. But then, he thought, it mightn't be all that bad if he knew the truth. He was only one person anyway. It wasn't as if the whole class was sitting there, listening.

"Me Dad's on the Dole, sir", he blurted out.

Although it made him feel wretched, he was glad he'd got it out and over with. The admission, however, didn't seem to affect Mr Henry, who simply said, "Oh, is he?"

He then asked what his job was when he was working, and when he told him he used to go away to sea, he seemed surprised and said he thought his Dad might have been an office worker or something.

As he began writing something down, Mr Henry said, "Well look here, Connolly, I'm going to give you ten out of ten for that poem, so you know what that means don't you?"

"No, sir."

"Well, Cassidy's was the highest before you. He got nine of out of ten. So that means you've come top."

Feeling a rare sense of pride, he wanted to thank the teacher, but he felt too awkward. It would have been too embarrassing to say thank you to somebody like a teacher.

Putting down his pen, Mr Henry said, "Tell me, what other poetry does your father recite?"

Sensing his interest, perhaps even his admiration, Sheridan suddenly became very proud of his Dad, because it was only through him that Mr Henry was being so kind. But still feeling uneasy with this new-found intimacy between himself and a grown-up, he quietly replied, "He knows lots sir, but I can't remember them all."

"Of course not", he said delicately, "but does he quote any Shakespeare, for instance?"

He thought for a few seconds then said, "Yes, sir. I think there's one about a bare bodkin or something like that. I think me Dad said that was by Shakespeare."

Then fearing he might be asked to recite it, he quickly added, "But that's a long one sir, I can't properly remember it all. And there's another long one about a man cutting exactly a pound of meat. I think me Dad said that was Shakespeare as well. But I don't know that one either."

Touching the stem of his glasses with a smile, the portly, balding Mr Henry began to quietly recite: *"Therefore prepare thee to cut off the flesh. But in the cutting if thou should shed one drop of Christian blood..."*

"That's it, sir!" he cried excitedly.

It was amazing to hear those intimate familiar words of his Dad's, which he'd never heard outside the four walls of their house, being spoken by another grown-up. But coming from Mr Henry, the words sounded posher and somehow seemed strange. It didn't make him feel the same as when his Dad spoke them, with his gestures and emotion and everything.

"How old are you now, Connolly?" asked Mr Henry, who now seemed even more interested.

"I was ten last July, sir ", he replied, once again feeling apprehensive of the teacher's curiosity.

"Well, those lines your father recites about the pound of flesh are from a play by William Shakespeare called, *The Merchant of Venice*. Now perhaps when you get a little older you may like to read some Shakespeare yourself, I dare say?"

Not knowing how to respond to this, Sheridan simply nodded in some kind of expectation - of exactly what, he didn't know.

"Are there any books you can read at home?" said the teacher. "Shakespeare, for instance?"

"No, sir", he replied.

These continual questions seemed like an interrogation. He wished it would stop and he could go out to play with the rest of them. Playtime, he thought, will be over by the time he's finished.

That reminded him: although he was Cock of the Class, he could imagine what the others out in the playground were already thinking, and the names they must be calling him, names like "teacher's pet," "posh arse" and "cissy". They wouldn't dare say anything to his face though.

"Well look here, Connolly", he went on, "I have quite a few small poetry books at home - Shakespeare, Keats, Longfellow and a few others. Do you like Longfellow?"

The teacher's manner seemed friendly and kind, but Sheridan still felt very embarrassed at this intimacy and the way he was talking to him almost as a grown-up equal.

"I don't know, sir", he replied awkwardly.

"Well, I'll bring them in tomorrow, and you can take them home with you. Would you like to do that?"

"What do yer mean, sir? Do yer mean to *keep*?"

"Yes, I'd like you to have them for your own. I think you will enjoy them a great deal. Not so much now perhaps, as when you get a little older."

Then, as if to finally convince himself, he added, "You *do* like poetry don't you?"

It seemed that he had overlooked this cardinal point and wanted to remove any doubt.

"Yes, sir", he quickly replied, feeling guilty, because he wasn't as keen about poetry as he thought he was expected to be.

With a sense of accomplishment, Mr Henry said, "Very well then. But don't say anything to the rest of the class. This is just between you and me. Okay?"

"Yes, sir", he replied, feeling awkward and stupid for saying nothing but "yes, sir" all the time.

Before dismissing him, Mr Henry told him, because he had missed the best part of Playtime, he could go home that afternoon ten minutes earlier than the others.

The following day the teacher kept his promise. Asking Sheridan to stay behind at four o'clock, he handed him a small brown parcel tied with string.

When he arrived home, he couldn't wait to open it. Dashing upstairs, he ripped open the parcel as fast as he could to find several small thick books. They looked very old, and smelled musty, but their titles were engraved in beautiful gold lettering. They seemed as if they'd been very expensive to buy when they were new.

Later that night, when his Dad saw them, he told him they weren't first editions and, because of that, were worth nothing.

In the books were poems by Shelley, Keats, Shakespeare, Pope, Wordsworth, Byron and Longfellow. Sheridan felt full up just looking through them all. He didn't know where to start, and this worried him slightly, for Mr Henry might suddenly test him one day out of the blue by asking him to recite one of them. And it would have felt terrible not to have justified his interest in him, to say nothing of how ungrateful he would seem.

So far he hadn't read any of the books properly. He couldn't understand them, they seemed dull and way above his head. The only ones he recognised and liked were those he'd heard his Dad reciting. He was amazed and thrilled to see all those familiar words of his Dad's actually in a book. And he was glad that he could now find out all the proper names of the poems he'd heard so often. One thing disappointed him though; some of them were slightly different from the way his Dad had spoken them. Only small things like a different word here or a missing word there, but it saddened him, because he knew the book couldn't be wrong. And up till then his Dad had always been perfect.

Since that time, he'd often thought that Mr Henry must have puzzled his brains out wondering how his Dad knew all that poetry, yet he'd never asked him about that. But he was glad he hadn't, as he later found out. He'd never have been able to tell him. He would have died of shame if he'd had to tell him that his Dad had learned it all in prison.

Chapter Three

"Come on, Sherry. Gonna sing a song for yer Dad?"

He hated that name, but his Dad always called him by it. He thought it was a cissy's name. It made him feel like a silly little girl. Nobody else called him Sherry. If anyone in school did, he would immediately give them a smack. And his Mam, who hated nicknames, would always give anyone a telling off for calling him by it. But no matter what he or his Mam said, his Dad always called him Sherry.

Now sitting in the other old armchair, by the dead fire in the grate, his Dad had recovered from *Sonny Boy* and had grown cheerful again. "Come on", he coaxed, "come on. Give us *I Wonder Who's Kissing Her Now?* Come on, just one song for yer Dad." He was truly shy about singing in front of anyone - even his Mam and Dad - but it didn't stop him now from cashing in on his shyness.

"Can I have another cup of ale then?" he asked, knowing his Dad wouldn't say no. He wouldn't refuse anyone anything when he was drunk. "Go on, have another cupful of ale" he said. And as Sheridan emptied the remains of the beer into the cracked cup, his Dad reached over to the other armchair and once more began prodding his Mam, telling her, "Hey Kate, come on girl. Come on, Sherry's gonna give us a song." Raising her head wearily, she mumbled, "Go away, leave me alone", then slumped back in the chair. But he kept prodding her.

Aware that this was the kind of situation which caused trouble to start, Sheridan began to sing, in the hope his Dad would stop prodding her. But he'd no sooner started when he heard a whistle at the front door's letter box. He knew it was Thomas by the tune. Thomas always whistled the first bit of *Bless 'Em All*. It was a sort of code they'd all built up without even thinking about it. When Brendan was home, he knew it couldn't be anybody else at the door when he'd hear *Run Rabbit Run*, because that was his "signature tune".

"That's Thomas!" he cried, partly out of surprise and partly for his Dad's benefit, before dashing along the lobby to open the front door. He'd had too many smacks across the face for keeping Thomas waiting!

When he was alone in the house and Thomas whistled, he'd have to wait and close the front door behind him like some servant. But now because his Mam and Dad were here, even though they were drunk, he ran back along the lobby leaving Thomas to close it himself. But, before he reached the kitchen, he heard the quiet but sinister sounding voice, "Getting brave cos me Mam and Dad's in, are we?" But sensing he had the edge - even if only temporarily - he replied, "Me Dad's gonna kill you! I told him about yer, about what yer done to me tonight. And he's drunk!" In truth he hadn't told his Dad anything, but he thought Thomas deserved to suffer for a change – even if only for a little while.

His Dad now seemed to have forgotten all about *I Wonder Who's Kissing Her Now?* He was more interested in where Thomas had been. Sheridan was glad he'd forgotten because deep down he didn't really like singing in front of anyone. It wasn't too bad when his Dad and Mam were drunk. It kind of gave him the courage he needed, because they never noticed when he sometimes got the words mixed up or sang slightly out of tune. But it was totally different in front of someone sober - especially if it was Thomas. He would always make fun of him later in bed, calling him a "fuckin' little show-off". At those times he felt really wretched because, despite his shyness, he was secretly proud of his singing voice. The trouble was, he thought, he only seemed to sound really good when he was on his own in the house. He could really let himself go then without feeling awkward and half-hearted, like he did singing in front of people.

When he was alone, especially during the light summer nights, he'd often go to the top of the stairs, right at the very top of the house, where it was spacious and the light came through the big skylight high above. At those times, he'd stand on the top landing and sing all the songs he knew. And because the stairs were bare wood and the two attic rooms had long ago lost their doors to his Dad for firewood, his voice would echo up the huge void to the skylight, back down and around through the attics, then down the four flights of stairs and back up again. It made him sound great. He'd heard of people singing in the bathroom and used to wish they had a bathroom. That would have been really great! But, he thought, singing up there was just as good as any bathroom.

One balmy Friday evening in the summer, he came home from the Hopey after seeing a Mario Lanza film, and although it was late it was still light at the top of the stairs. There was nobody in the house, so he climbed the stairs to the top landing and, beneath the skylight, started singing *Be My Love*. And the more he became lost in the song, the more he began to believe that he was actually Mario Lanza. He'd been going full blast at that time when he suddenly heard *Bless `Em All* being whistled along the lobby downstairs. Knowing who it was, he deliberately lowered his voice and began singing out of tune. That was how non-singing people sang, he thought, so if Thomas had heard him, he couldn't accuse him of fancying himself as a singer. But Thomas wasn't so easily deceived, nor was he deaf. He'd heard the singing, and when Sheridan dashed down to open the front door, he called him all the stupid bastards under the sun for singing to himself. So nowadays he only pretended to be Nat King Cole, because *Mona Lisa* and songs like that were a lot quieter to sing and much harder for anybody else to hear - especially when he'd cup one hand around his mouth and the other around his ear. Not only did this amplify the sound for himself, it also ensured that nobody else could hear him.

A worried expression appeared on Thomas's face when he saw the state of his Mam in the armchair. "What's wrong with her?" he asked.

"She's alright", said his Dad. "Don't worry about yer mother. She's had a load of ale. She's bevvied." He seemed to be proud of her helpless, drunken state. Looking less worried now, he asked if his Dad wanted a cup of tea.

"No, yer alright lad", he replied, "I'm aces. Me and yer mother have had a bellyful of ale. Don't worry about us. But you'se muck in yourselves if there's any scoff in the cupboard." Then patting his stomach, he added, "Me and yer mother's chocker."

Glancing at the empty kettle on the gas stove, Thomas shot Sheridan a meaningful glance. If his Dad hadn't been here, he knew who would have had to go and fill it. But now he quickly looked away and Thomas, not wanting to upset his drunken Dad, picked up the kettle and went downstairs. After he'd gone, Sheridan deliberately closed the kitchen door, so that when he came back across the cellar, he'd have no chink of light to guide him up the stairs.

Now slumped in the chair, his Dad was becoming drowsy, his chin sagging on his chest. When Thomas returned with the kettle of water, he roared at Sheridan, "Yer little bastard! What did yer close the door for? Yer know I can't see in the fuckin' dark!" Adopting an innocent expression, but secretly laughing inside, he pretended he'd forgotten. But it was nice to know his brother was as scared of the cellar as he was.

Thomas's shouting caused his Dad to stir. "What's going on?" he muttered. Sounding really hurt, he cried, "This stupid bleeder closed the door on me. I couldn't see me way back up the apples."

"Well, yer should've took the candle with yer", said his Dad. "Use yer fuckin' brains!" When he complained he'd cracked his shin in the dark cellar, Sheridan was even more pleased, even though he knew he'd get a few punches in the back when they were in bed. Thomas always punched him in the back, because it hardly ever bruises. And even when it does, the bruises can't so easily be seen.

By now his Dad seemed to be sobering up. He'd even drank the cup of tea Thomas gave him, and was now back on his feet standing in front of the fireplace singing again, but now lower and sweeter. The song, *Go To Sleep My Little Drummer Boy*, was another that Sheridan really liked. But Thomas wasn't impressed at all. He seemed to have become bored long ago with his Dad's singing.

Thomas knew the boring routine only too well. When the singing stopped it then used to be "shirts off" for himself and

Brendan, whilst his Dad flexed his muscles and did all sorts of physical exercises, telling them to copy him. Then when they were exhausted it would be "sex time". That was when his Dad started telling them dirty jokes and how, no matter how nice-looking some women were, they still pissed and shit like men and that you could catch the pox from them. He was so disgusting, it seemed he must have really hated women. He never seemed to be embarrassed when he was drunk. And it always made him feel terrible to think about that because there were several girls he liked - and one he was particularly fond of - but when he was in their company, although he tried not to think of it, he couldn't keep such things out of his mind, and he always ended up feeling miserable and disgusted.

Mad hungry after sitting in the *Palais-de-Luxe* for four hours, he began searching for some bread in the small cupboard in the sideboard, which was used as a small larder. But there was only a rock-hard quarter of a loaf, which had been there for days. "No bleedin' bread again", he murmured angrily. "It's getting fuckin' worse in this house." Then, turning to Sheridan, he said, "D'yer know if she's got a loaf planted anywhere?"

"I don't know", he replied, as his Dad carried on singing '*Drummer Boy*. "Go and look in the coal cupboard", ordered Thomas, pointing to the door in the corner of the room.

Although it was now where rubbish and the weekly coal supply was dumped, this had originally been the larder. Their Mam often hid a loaf or tin of Spam in there under the rubbish on one of the shelves. She was always hiding things around the house - especially food. It was the war which had made her like that. She'd got so used to things being so scarce, she couldn't get out of the habit of hoarding everything in case they ran short. Apart from several short trips to sea, their Dad had mostly been on the Dole all through the war. And she'd had a hard enough time feeding them on just the National Assistance Board money, without everything being rationed as well. And, although she'd had five ration books, they couldn't afford luxuries like butter and cheese and meat, so she used to sell her ration coupons to Annie Silver, the moneylender. Annie was a widow with no children and only had one ration book. But she had plenty of money, so she could afford butter and steak and things like that.

Standing on the heap of coal in the cupboard, Sheridan felt his way along the top shelf where she usually hid things. Pushing aside the old wooden box full of old photographs and documents, and the rusty National Dried Milk tins filled with buttons and pins and cotton reels, he spotted it wrapped in newspaper - a large farmhouse loaf. As he eagerly grabbed it, he felt a tickling sensation on the back of his hand, and although he couldn't see properly in the murky cupboard, he knew it was a mouse. The house was full of them. Shuddering with fright and nausea, he staggered backwards in sheer panic, knocking over the old wooden box as he did so, causing it to spill its contents over the pile of coal.

"What the fuckin'ell are yer doin' in there? Get out've there!" roared his Dad, who was angry not only at the noise, but also at his sweet song being interrupted. Sheridan was now trembling but managed to keep hold of the loaf as he staggered out of the cupboard. Thomas was pleased to see the bread and even more pleased to see his brother being shouted at, and pointing to his temple, he told his Dad, "He's round the fuckin' bend, he is." Ignoring Thomas, his Dad asked, "Have yer knocked yer grandad's box over?"

Not wanting them to know he was scared of the mouse, Sheridan said he'd accidentally slipped on the coal.

"Well, go an' pick it up", shouted Thomas, "and put everything back!" But his Dad said, "Don't worry about it. Worse things happen at sea."

Knowing how dangerously unsafe the cupboard floor was through having hundred-weights of coal thrown on it every Saturday morning, he was relieved Sheridan hadn't fallen through to the cellar below. "Are yer alright lad?" he asked. His changed, concerned manner made Sheridan feel more relaxed. "Yeah, I'm okay", he replied, bracing himself to ignore the mice and go back in.

Before picking up its scattered contents, he quickly retrieved the empty box and placed it on the kitchen table then returned with a lighted candle to the cupboard. But as he squatted on the coal gathering up the box's contents, his Dad, now examining the box, called him out.

If it hadn't been black with age and dirt, the box could have been mistaken for a First Aid box. It had a small keyhole near the hinged lid and an inset on the inside, where at one time there had been a lock.

"D'yer see that box?" said his Dad as Thomas began cutting himself a thick slice of bread, "well that was yer grandad's that was. Been all over the world that has. New York, Boston, Panama, Santa Marta South America, Sydney, Australia, Savannah Georgia. Everywhere that's been. If it could talk it wouldn't half have some tales to tell."

Gazing at the box, Sheridan thought his Dad seemed much warmer now, as he tried to share the past with them. But Thomas only looked at it because he was expected to. He was too hungry to be bothered about some dirty, raggedy old box. "D'yiz know where that'd be now only for fate?" he went on. Unlike his brother, Sheridan was eager to know where the box would be. "The bottom of the Atlantic. That's where it would be", said his Dad.

Sitting on the wooden chair, with his elbows on the table and his hands cupping his chin, Sheridan was fascinated. "Why, Dad?" he asked. His posture and expression brought an admiring grin to his Dad's face. Turning to Thomas, he said. "Look at him. *The Boyhood of Raleigh*, eh. *The Boyhood of Raleigh*."

Thomas didn't know what he was talking about. Neither did Sheridan, but he somehow sensed, by his Dad's proud expression, that it was something good about him. But suddenly feeling uneasy, his face, despite his struggle to control it, began to blush bright red, and he was glad when his Dad started talking again.

"Haven't yiz ever seen the painting of Sir Walter Raleigh, when he was a kid?" he asked. And before they could reply he went on, "Yiz wanna go down the *Walker Art Gallery* and have a look at it. It shows the old seafaring fella pointing out to sea and talking to the young Raleigh, when he was a kid. And yer can see the look of wonder on the kid's face. That's how he came to explore the world when he became a man. Yiz wanna go and see it. It's an education."

Although the story of Raleigh was interesting, Sheridan was more interested in the grimy wooden box on the table. "Hey Dad", he said, "finish off telling us about the box."

"Well", he said, "yer grandad, yer mother's father, that was his Diddy Box. All the seamen in those days had one to carry their belongings in. Yer know, discharge papers and documents and that. Anyway", he went on, "yer grandad went away for years. He was a stoker on the old White Star and Cunard boats. All the stokers and trimmers and fireman were big strong men, they couldn't half fight. Yer had to be hard in those days. Either that, or yer led a dog's life at sea."

Sheridan was enjoying the tale, but his enjoyment was tinged with regret that his grandad had died before he was born. Even Thomas, he noticed, was now interested for a change. Usually, he was never interested in anything except John Wayne and girls.

"Anyway", continued his Dad, "like I said, he sailed in all the best ships, the *Britannic*, the *Mauritania*, the *Georgic*, *Canopic*, *Celtic*, *Aquitania*, *Adriatic*, the lot. Well, he was getting on a bit, when he got the wire to join the *Titanic*, in Southampton for its maiden voyage. God blimey, she was a beautiful specimen of a ship, she was! 'The Unsinkable' they called her, and God blimey, she looked it!"

By now both Sheridan and Thomas were engrossed in the story as he continued. "Well, yer grandad had never missed a ship in his life. No matter how drunk he'd be the night before - and he could bevvy! He'd always turn to, hail, rain or snow. And the best thing about signing on for the *Titanic*, he really thought it was a honour to sail on the greatest ship in the world on her first trip."

Hypnotised by the glamour and adventure of it all, almost tasting the romance and freedom of the sea, Sheridan vowed there and then to himself that someday he too would go away to sea. But something was nagging at him. Why did his Dad say his grandad only "thought" it was an honour? Surely, he asked, it was an honour to be one of the crew of the greatest ship in the world? "There was no honour in them ships", said his Dad. "Down below yer worked like a slave. That's why they were so tough, those firemen. There was none of yer oil-firing in those days. All steamers, coal burners they were, and yer worked yer balls off till the sweat rolled off yer. I'll tell yiz something", he went on, "when yer came off watch after firing eight hours down below, yer body would be aching all over and you'd be dehydrated. Yer always had to work stripped to the waist. If yer was stupid enough to wear a singlet, it would be so drenched with sweat after a few minutes, yer could use it as a wet flannel. And yer always had to wear yer belt back to front to stop the buckle getting red hot and burning yer bare belly. And yer know how much yer got? You'd be lucky if yer got ten pound a month. And to put the top hat on it, the least little thing yer did wrong, yer got logged a week's money."

As hard and cruel as this all sounded to Sheridan, none of it left as deep an impression as all those far away, romantic-sounding places like Savannah Georgia, Santa Marta and Panama.

"Anyhow, as I was saying", continued his Dad, "the only reason that box is not lying at the bottom of the ocean is because two nights before he was due to join the *Titanic* in Southampton, yer grandad got pinched in Scotland Road. In the *Athol* alehouse it was, comer of Athol Street. He'd been on the ale all day. Anyway, some gink tried to take a liberty with him. He was a lot younger, this fella, but yer grandad put him asleep with the old one-two-three." His chin still cupped in his palms, Sheridan was now totally absorbed, as his Dad went on. "Well, after he'd dropped this gink, he was trying to get out of the place as quick as he could, when a team comes from nowhere. Must have been the fella's mates. Then he had a real Battle Royal. Anyway, the coppers took him to the Royal Infirmary to get all the blood off, then took him down to the Bridewell and charged him with assault and being drunk."

By now Thomas was equally fascinated with the tale. "Anyway", said his Dad, now lighting up his last dog-end, "he was charged with doing the gink and two of the team, and the alehouse manager, so there was no chance of bail. Well, he caused fuckin' murder in the cells in Cheapside! Even the coppers were scared of him, because he was known as a hard case around Scotland Road. In the court the next morning, he got three months gaol and, when he realised he wasn't gonna get out to join the *Titanic*, he cried his heart out like a baby, as big as he was. And that's no kiddin'."

"Well", said a puzzled Thomas, "wasn't the *Titanic* the one that got sunk?"

"Yeah, the icebergs got her off Cape Race, Newfoundland. Opened up like a fuckin' tin of sardines she did. Hundreds went down on her." Still looking puzzled Thomas said, "Well, in that case, that means me grandad would have been killed as well."

"Oh aye yeah, definitely", he replied without feeling. "That's what I mean. What kind of honour would that have been? Wouldn't have stood a fuckin' dog's chance. The poor bastards down below were the first to get it. Right down in the bowels of the ship yer are, and when she rips like the *Titanic* did there's scalding steam everywhere. Yer trapped like bleedin' rats."

The dog-end now smoked, he pulled out a packet of cigarette papers and began "dusting out" his pockets of tobacco dust to try and roll another cigarette. It was mostly dirt and bits of fluff, but there were quite a few grains of tobacco too. Then, lighting the thin, queer-shaped object, he went on, "The 'Lucy' was the same. She was torpedoed off Ireland a few years later by the Germans. Loads of Liverpool stokers and trimmers went down on her too. Died some terrible deaths them men did."

Sheridan saw the panic vividly and smelled the scalding flesh and heard the agonising screams, as though he'd actually been there himself in the thick of it. But it still never dissuaded him from wanting to go away to sea when he grew up.

Thomas, said he couldn't understand why his Dad was more interested in the old dirty box, rather than his grandad's narrow escape from drowning on the *Titanic*. Glancing wryly at him before returning his gaze to the box, he said, "The *Titanic's* at the bottom of the ocean now, dead and buried like yer grandad. And that's one thing we can all be certain of - the Bury Hole. But that box, that's still here, isn't it? And it'll probably be here when I'm dead and gone. And even when you'se are in yer graves, it'll most likely still be there in one of yer son's or daughter's coal-cupboards. That's a lot better than lying rotting at the bottom of the ocean, isn't it? I wouldn't wish that on me biggest enemy."

There was silence for a few moments. Then, gazing fondly at the box again, he said, "To look at it yer wouldn't think it was fifty odd, would yer? When he first got it, it was white and brand spanking new. Willow that is. Lasts for years that stuff does."

Sheridan and Thomas were now feeling tired. But each knew their Dad wouldn't understand. He never did when he wanted to carry on talking. He always said that, if something was worth talking about, it was worth listening to. And true to form, with a stern expression replacing the warmth and wistfulness of a few moments ago, he suddenly turned nasty towards Sheridan, whose eyelids by now were drooping. "What the fuckin'ell's wrong with you?" he sneered.

Feeling the sudden fear creeping over him, he quickly pulled himself together. Although his Dad never hit him, he sometimes thought he might have preferred being hit to these insults and mockery, which were always so sudden and unexpected.

"Listen, you little prick", he continued, "yer wanna stop playing with yer fuckin' self. That's why yer tired and got no fuckin' energy."

His face now burning with shock and embarrassment, he cried indignantly, "I don't, Dad."

"Yis yer do. Don't try and kid yer father." He felt wretched and helpless, but his Dad wouldn't relent. "I've told yer before, yer silly little cunt. If yer start playing with yerself, you'll end up blind and all yer hair'll fall out, and you'll end up in the fuckin' lunatic asylum. D'yer wanna grow up to be a fuckin' idiot and a weakling, do yer?"

Sheridan was lost for words. Not only because of the sudden change in his Dad, and his embarrassment in front of Thomas, but also because he knew his Dad had guessed right. But he never did it as often these days - not since he had first warned him last year.

It always puzzled him how his Dad knew because nobody ever saw him. He only ever did it when he was alone in the house. He thought that perhaps his Dad didn't really know for sure and that he was just bluffing him. Or that maybe he was so sure because he knew his own tricks best from when he was a kid himself.

He remembered the first time last year when his Dad had told him and Thomas that you could always tell when anyone had been "tossing off", as he'd called it, because hairs started growing on the palms of your hands. The memory of it was so painful, even now when he recalled how guilty he'd felt when his Dad had caught him sneakily looking at his hands. But he also remembered feeling a little better when he saw Thomas doing the same, because until then he'd never thought other, bigger lads did things like that - especially his brother. He'd always thought that it was only himself, and that he must be some sort of freak. It had come as a real shock to find that even Thomas did it, so perhaps he wasn't a freak after all. And for a while, although this had made him feel a lot better, it seemed to make Thomas pitful. But his brother didn't seem at all pitiful now when, to his dismay, he joined in the attack.

"You're stupid yer know. Yer wanna stop doing that,", he lectured, trying to keep the focus off himself. But his Dad didn't fall for the diversion. "That goes for you as well", he said turning on him. "Saps all yer fuckin' strength. You'll end up a fuckin' idiot."

Trying to look manly, he cried indignantly, "I don't bleedin' well do it. I can get as many girls as I like." But, if the truth was known, Thomas had never had a girl in his life.

On the verge of tears through the dirt and shame of it all, Sheridan said, "Where's the candle? I'm going to bed."

"What's yer hurry?" demanded his Dad. "No school in the morning is there?" Still fearful but thinking his Dad would be pleased at him showing some initiative, he said almost in whisper, "I know. But I wanna get up early. Me and me mate's going downtown to the market to get some wood to sell."

Sheridan had always been able to forage for himself by doing errands for neighbours or shifting snow or collecting rags and jam jars or selling firewood. He'd had to because he never got any pocket money. But his Dad wasn't impressed. "Well", he said contrarily, "the market doesn't open till nine o'clock, does it?"

"I know that", he replied, "but we wanna get down to the fruit market in Queen's Square, and *they* open about six o'clock in the morning. We wanna get there first 'cos other lads from around here go down there of a Saturday and they'll get all the boxes, if we don't get there before them."

Sensing his Dad was stumped, he felt triumphant. Thomas knew it and he thought if his Mam, still drunkenly slouched in the chair, had been awake, she would have known it too. He'd got his own back on his Dad for making him feel so wretched and guilty.

Carrying the lighted candle up the stairs, he felt like crying. But, resisting the temptation, he instead whispered to himself, "Dirty drunken old bastard!"

Hours later, lying at the foot of the bed in the darkened room, he was awakened by a low droning sound. But it wasn't Thomas with his usual snoring. It was his Dad downstairs quietly singing, *When I'm Gone You'll Soon Forget Me*.

Chapter Four

In the event, Sheridan never got up early after all. He was awake most of the night dreading the moment when his Dad would finally stop singing and, as always, come to bed and wake his Mam up. But last night when he came to bed, Sheridan heard his Mam mumbling and telling him to fuck off. And funnily enough, he never belted her like he usually did. He didn't even answer her back. He just kept on quietly singing some old Irish songs. But it still took Sheridan ages to feel safe enough to drop off to sleep.

When he awoke it was late, about half-eleven he guessed, because he could hear all the traffic and hustle and bustle from the main road a few yards up the street. He could also hear the banging and hammering coming from Metweld, the metal workshop in the garage across the street - and they hardly ever came in before eleven o'clock on a Saturday morning. So, although he couldn't see anything through the one window-pane that wasn't boarded up with cardboard, he just knew it was dead late and that he'd better get up right away.

Putting on his trousers and grabbing his boots and socks, he leapt down the stairs two at a time to the smoke-filled kitchen, where his Mam was frying kippers. He didn't know why, but they always had kippers on Saturday mornings. His Dad was sitting unwashed and unshaven in the old armchair reading yesterday's *Daily Mail*. He was glad it was the *'Mail* instead of the *Daily Mirror* or *Herald*, because when his Dad finished with it, he could read the Rip Kirby comic strip as usual.

"You'll have to wait till me and yer father have ours", said his Mam, placing two plates of kippers on the table. He didn't know why she even bothered saying that, he always had to wait until they'd had theirs anyway.

His Dad looked terrible, he thought. He badly needed a shave, and his black hair, which was going grey at the sides, was all wild and woolly, and when it was like that it showed up the bald patch on the top of his head. And the old, round-necked, singlet he was wearing with buttons up the front, looked like an army one and made him look thin and scrawny. You definitely wouldn't have guessed it was the same Dad as last night, he thought, as he sat in the opposite armchair putting on his socks and boots.

Neither of them said anything about the market. His Mam, because she knew nothing about it, and his Dad had been too drunk last night to remember anything. Instead, fumbling in his trouser pocket, he suddenly ordered, "Hurry up and get yer shoes and socks on, and go round to McDonough's and get me a blue Gillette razor blade and five Woodbines." He was in a grumpy mood as always the morning after the ale - especially if he had no cigarettes.

Nervously trying to get his socks on, it occurred to Sheridan that no matter how drunk his Dad was the night before, or no matter how late he went to bed, he would always be up at eleven o'clock the next morning. His Mam always said that it was because he wanted to be ready for half-eleven when the pubs opened, but he thought it must be something more than that. But what, he didn't know.

Sheridan was now hurriedly folding the toes of the big woollen socks underneath, so they wouldn't start flapping out of the big rips at the front of his boots when he was running to McDonough's shop. The problem was, the soles had come apart from the welts, and the toes of his socks were almost threadbare through him treading on them through the torn, gaping, flapping boots. It made him so mad because it always took him so long to get ready, especially when he was late for school. And when it was raining it was even worse. He would try and walk on his heels, but before long, his ankles would start aching and, by the time he got to school, he'd given up trying to keep his feet dry. By then they would be freezing cold, sodden, and squelching with the wetness. But, as bad as that was, the worst thing was the shame when some of the teachers would look at him with disgust. Sometimes some of the kids would start laughing, but he always belted any he caught. If any of the older ones laughed though, he just had to put up with it, because he could only fight the kids in his class or those below. He often thought how stupid and unfair it was that he, the Cock of the Class, had to come to school like this, whilst all the other gutless little bastards were always so well dressed.

There was only one other kid in his class as poor as himself and that was "Sloppy Joe" Flaherty, from Paddington, who had been given the nickname because he was always so scruffy. He was really bad. He'd sometimes come to school in a girl's coat to hide the big holes in his short pants. And his shoes became so bad through him always tripping over and cutting and bruising himself, that one day he came to school wearing a pair of light-brown women's shoes. The heels weren't that high, but in the playground all the kids were laughing their heads off just the same. Sheridan had thumped a few of those he could fight, but he couldn't stop the bigger lads from their teasing. He felt really sorry for Flaherty. He'd even thought once about making a friend of him. But he quickly realised it wouldn't have worked because everybody knew Flaherty was backward, and he didn't want to get "tarred with the same brush" as his Dad used to say.

If his Mam could get him another pair from the Secondhand shop, thought Sheridan wistfully, there'd be no need for all this messing around. But whenever he asked her, she'd either say she couldn't afford them, or that it served him right for kicking tin cans in the street all the time when she'd told him not to.

After finally getting the flaps tucked in, he dashed around the corner to McDonough's. His Dad always sent him there for cigarettes, because Mrs McDonough, who knew his Mam and Dad well, would sell them from "under the counter", without coupons. She even sold him sweets and toffee from under the counter.

Before dashing to the shop, he'd never thought about getting a wash and nobody told him to. None of them ever got a wash before their breakfast. With only the kettle to heat the cold water from the tap in the cellar, it was a case of first things first: cups and plates, or hands and faces. The only one in the family who always washed first thing of a morning was Brendan, when he was home. And even he had only begun to since he'd been in the army.

When Sheridan had left for the shop, his Mam said, "Come on, Frank, are yer sitting down to these?" Sitting himself at the table, he said with a worried look, "Yer know what, Kate? If I had the coppers, I could get some leather and tacks and sole and heel them boots for him. Fuckin' hard luck on the poor kid havin' to go around like that. He'll end up getting pneumonia." But taking this as an accusation against herself, she cried defensively, "Don't you be talkin'. How do yer think I feel?" Then, her anger rising, she went on, "If you'd leave the fuckin' money alone out of the gas meter, I might be able to do something for the poor child." This was the only time she could get the edge on him - when he was sober. And he knew it. "Oh don't fuckin' start again", he sighed painfully. "I will start", she cried defiantly. "You're sickening for a man. You're not fuckin' natural. Ale, ale, ale, that's all yer ever think of. And when yer can't bum any more, yer start robbing yer own gas meter. Yer can't get any lower than that!" Her expression was one of disgust, but he immediately hit back. "You needn't talk", he cried. "What are you getting on yer high horse for? You got your fuckin' share didn't yer?"

"Too bleedin' true", she shouted back. "And why shouldn't I? I'll be the one who ends up paying it back like always, so why shouldn't I get a drink out of it?"

Realising she was on weak ground, she changed her line of attack and began goading him. "What's up", she jeered sarcastically, "goin' mad because yer couldn't have it all yerself to treat yer fancy women with down the town?" With a look of exasperation, he cried, "How many times have do I have to tell yer, I'm not fuckin' interested in other women!" But ignoring his protestations, she kept up the taunting. "Go on now", she mocked. "Yer don't fuckin' say now." Then reverting to her earlier disgust, she quietly said, "Go away you poxy drunkard. You make me fuckin' sick." Her contempt left him lost for words, making him feel small and at her mercy. But what could he do? Finally get it over with and kill her? What would that solve? If she were dead, he thought, he wouldn't even be able to command her respect. And that's all he had ever wanted - her respect.

A deep hatred towards women suddenly bubbled inside him. So petty, the bastards! So damaging to an intelligent man like himself. And her scorn always cut him so deeply. She knew how to wound alright. A few lines of a poem he'd learned in prison suddenly came to him:

"Though rash actions can rupture a friendship,

harsh words can carry more bite.

A blow can be quickly forgotten,

whilst words are prolonged in the fight."

He couldn't remember who had written it but, he thought, that gink really knew about women. The way they always managed to drag you down to their petty, bitching level. The only thing they understood was a fuckin' good hiding!

Suddenly, she broke in on his silent brooding. "Well, I'll tell yer something right now", she declared, "That child's gonna have a new pair of shoes. He's gone without for long enough, and you won't do fuck all for him."

Deep down, he knew she was a good mother. One of the best, she was. She'd sooner starve herself than see any of the kids go short. He was glad to hear what she'd just said, but it also made him feel even smaller. What kind of a husband and a father was he? He was supposed to be the main provider, the Man of the House, wasn't he? The trouble was he'd run out of ideas for getting a few quid. All the strokes had been pulled too often. How many times is the N.A.B. going to swallow that you've lost your allowance money and pay you again? He'd pulled that one more times than he could remember. The last time he tried it they just gave him food vouchers and told him he wouldn't even get them if he made another phony claim. But as bad as the situation was now, he was proud of how often he'd fooled them. His performances, he thought wistfully, were so good he would have won umpteen Academy Awards if he'd been in pictures: especially when he'd cry real tears and pull his hair out in front of those officials. But then again, he thought, if he'd been in pictures getting all those Oscars, he wouldn't have had to go begging to the National Assistance Board in the first place.

He was even played out at the Soldiers & Sailors & Airforce Association and the Royal Air Force Benevolent Fund. He'd tapped them so often, they wouldn't give him any more grants. They'd finally told him there were men who had been in the services for years, even Victoria Cross and Military Medal holders who'd never asked them for a penny in their lives, never mind an RAF rookie who'd never even seen any action, and who'd only joined up when the war was practically over. In the circumstances he reckoned he'd done very good to have gotten so much out of them, considering how much he'd hated the Airforce and how he'd worked his ticket after three months.

The British Legion was another one whose black books he was in. He couldn't go near them anymore for the same reason. There wasn't even a "compo" case coming up, which he could borrow some money on the strength of - and there was nearly always one of them in the offing. It had been a good fiddle, the compo lark. But old Jasper Deakin, the solicitor, had warned him to lay off for a while. What with a case nearly every month, he'd told him they were pushing it a bit too much and it was getting too hot. It seemed their regular claims against shops and companies were going back to the same few insurance firms, who were becoming very suspicious. Still, he thought, it had been good while it lasted. Kate was usually the one who was supposed to have tripped over the dangerous grid outside a pub, or eaten a so-called green mouldy piece of cake bought fresh that day from the confectioners. But she wasn't a very good actress. He always had to be there, usually as a "witness", or simply as her husband to explain what had happened and to see that everything went smoothly, that she played her part authentically and didn't slip up and ruin the whole act. Old Deakin did all right out of it too. He always got his cut, and his costs. In fact, he'd done better out of it than him and Kate put together. But then, he did represent them for free, taking a chance on whether or not the other side would settle out of court. Still, he thought, never mind. If Deakin said spew it for now, then spew it he would. He wasn't a solicitor for nothing, and he always respected brains. In any case, all wasn't lost. When Deakin gave him the green light, they could always have another go. Trouble was, he thought, how long will that be?

What angered him more than anything else, was the way Kate would scorn and despise him when things got a bit rough, like now. She didn't half have a short memory, he thought. It was a different story altogether when they'd be in the money after a good compo case. She'd be all over him then, when he'd take her out downtown and buy her a new coat and shoes, and take her to McManus's for Guinness and cockles and oysters, and then take her on a tour of all the city-centre pubs. They'd have some really great times, but he would always first make sure he gave her enough money to stock up with food and make sure the kids were clothed.

Sometimes, when he really wanted to impress her, and to avoid bumping into any of his drunken cronies, he'd take her to the old-fashioned, classy pubs, the *Pig & Whistle* or the *Pen & Wig*, in the posh, commercial part of town where all the *educated* people drank. He'd often meet old Deakin and have a celebration drink with him. But even if he didn't meet him, he would invariably end up in conversation with a barrister or solicitor or an office bigwig - which made him feel proud and seemed to restore his self-esteem in front of Kate. And remembering all these positive things, these good things he'd done for his wife and family in past times, seemed to suddenly make him feel much better.

"Listen, Kate," he said apologetically, "Don't worry girl. Something'll turn up. Yer know me. If I'm not fishin', I'm mendin' me nets." She knew she couldn't argue with him there. It was true. But still and all, she hated this life of "up one minute and down the next". Why, she thought, couldn't he just be like any other *normal* husband and father. That wasn't too much to ask. Just for him to be normal and have a regular job like everyone else. For her to be able to get up every morning and make his breakfast before he left for work; to be doing her housework and shopping whilst he was at work all day; to feel warm and secure in the knowledge that he would be coming home each night to the nice hot meal she'd prepared for him, instead of coming home day and night, fighting or singing drunk - *that* was all she wanted. *That* would have made her the happiest woman on earth. But deep inside she knew he could never ever be like that. Since he'd packed up going away to sea six years ago, she'd given up asking him to get a job. He just wasn't the type.

The loud shattering of the front door being slammed shut broke the tense quiet, making them both jump with alarm. Young feet raced along the lobby until the kitchen door flew open and they saw Sheridan lying face down half-way in the doorway. The old worn boots had tripped him up once again.

"Hey, Dad", he panted, with a terrified expression, "the Gasman's coming up the street!" Aware his Dad had removed the lock and emptied the meter in the front cellar, he knew how serious the situation was. Quickly jumping to his feet, his Dad shouted, "Quick draw the curtains!" then immediately began drawing them himself. His Mam panicking, moaned, "Oh! my God!" then sat down, clasping her hands together so tightly that her knuckles became white with the tension. Looking thin and distraught, she began to tremble slightly. Despite the terror of the emergency, Sheridan tried to hide his amusement at the way his Dad had shouted, "draw the curtains", and then drew them himself. He knew why he drew the curtains of course. It was in case the Gasman came around the back entry and spied through the back yard door into the kitchen, which they sometimes did when they got no answer at the front. But his Dad's action made him laugh nevertheless.

As the three of them sat waiting, quiet as mice, his Mam and Dad in the two old armchairs and Sheridan on the old wooden chair with no back on it, his Dad was staring absently at him, his ears cocked like those of an alert cat, and it was so quiet, the sounds of their breathing resembled a blustery gale.

"Bang! Bang! Bang!" That was the old cast iron knocker on the front door he was using. The sound was really official. You could tell it was someone important, thought Sheridan, when you heard the knocker. It was frightening, because only the police or the landlord or the Gasman ever used it. No friend ever used it.

Sitting still as a rock, his Dad put a finger to his pursed lips and whispered "hush" to them, even though they weren't making a sound. "Bang! Bang! Bang!" This time it made Sheridan jump with fright. He felt sick and panicky like he did years ago when Freckles had him gripped by the collar and wouldn't let go. He feared the Gasman might stay there all day until somebody answered the door. And he was afraid that, if nobody did, the Gasman might even smash the front door down.

The silence in the kitchen continued. There had been no banging for several minutes. Sheridan, his fear gradually subsiding, relaxed a little and began to fidget on the old wooden chair because it was so hard.

"Bang! Bang! Bang!" He jumped again and felt the heavy ache of dread in his belly returning. It was like Freckles all right. The attack was remorseless. It wouldn't let up. And it was making him angry now as well as scared. When was it going to fuckin' stop?!

Apart from the distant traffic noises coming from the main road, and the more immediate noise from the Metweld garage across the street, it had become quiet once more. Sheridan had been trying to hold his breath from the beginning, and this had affected his throat, which now began to tickle annoyingly. Forcing himself not to swallow, he knew that the next time he swallowed the tickling sensation would be so great he wouldn't be able to stop himself from coughing.

The silence seemed to last for ages this time, so his Mam allowed herself the luxury of crossing her legs. But the rustling noise she made in the rickety old armchair caused his Dad to give her an angry, threatening look. Seeing this, Sheridan became too scared to budge. But through sitting in the upright hard chair, his back now began to ache, and the tickling in his throat was becoming worse. He craved for just one really good cough to get rid of it but knew that was out of the question. But suddenly, with a feeling of dreadful apprehension, he felt the tickle now growing from a faint, irritating pest into a tantalising, maddening, gigantic demon. Swallowing quickly, he tried to get rid of it once and for all, but as he did so his body shook uncontrollably and, to his horror, he heard himself loudly coughing. Unable to stop himself, he managed, despite the panic and dizziness, to stifle the noise by clamping both hands over his mouth. But peering fearfully over his hands at his Dad, he was met by a look of wild-eyed rage. His smoke-stained stained gaping teeth were bared in a murderous expression, as he snarled in a whisper, "You dirty little cunt!" Terrified, and overcome with guilt and shame, it seemed to Sheridan that he had betrayed them all.

"Bang! Bang! Bang!" He felt certain this was going to be a fight to the death! The Gasman *must* have known they were inside, the knocking was so insistent and emphatic.

Sheridan's palms were now soaking wet with anxiety, and the panic and nausea caused a foul taste in his mouth making him nearly vomit. "Please, mister", he pleaded desperately inside himself, "go away. Please! Please! Please! Go away!" By some miracle his prayers were finally answered because, although they waited and waited, the banging on the front door finally ceased.

It seemed an age since he'd ran into the kitchen and fallen over. But when he saw his Dad gingerly drawing back the curtains, he knew that at last the agony was over. And although his body felt stiff and cramped all over, it was great to feel safe and free again. And his Dad didn't say anything more about the coughing, which made him feel even better.

After finishing his kippers and bread and margarine, he went down to the cellar to get washed without feeling a bit scared. He never did in the daytime. He was going to call for his friend, Reggie Palmer, who lived next door but one. They were going down to the wholesale fruit market in Queen's Square today to collect as many orange boxes as they could haul back up the steep inclines of Leece Street and Hardman Street, to chop up and sell as firewood.

Chapter Five

A fter first going around the fruit merchants in Queen's
Square, where they got some orange and tomato boxes,
Sheridan and Reggie moved on to the fish market, where they
got more crates and boxes. But because these stank of fish and
were mostly soaking wet, they decided to dump them in the
alley at the rear of Lime Street. Wet wood was too hard to chop
up.

Next, they went around all the fruit barrows on the bombed
site opposite Blacklers department store until, finally, they had
much more firewood than they could handle. The problem was
that it was all different shaped boxes, with nails and wire and
loose bits of wood sticking out, so they now had to get it into
manageable form to drag it up the steep hill.

Keeping two large orange boxes intact, they smashed up the
remaining ones with their hands and feet and loaded the small
pieces into the two boxes, then attached two lengths of strong
string to the nails at the front of the boxes and began the long
haul home.

Thrilled with their success, Sheridan guessed they would
easily get their Hopey money out of this lot. And to make

things even better, their pockets were stuffed with the bruised and faded apples and oranges left in the boxes.

He loved Saturdays. He reckoned it was easily the best day of the week. No school for a start. Loads of free fades, and as much wood as you wanted, to sell for your picture money. It was great!

In this roasting hot weather, they were both drenched with sweat by the time they reached their street with the loads of wood. You could tell how hot it was by the odd patches of tar on the street's surface, which had begun to erupt into numerous tar bubbles.

When he was smaller, along with the other kids from the street, he would spend all day sitting in the hot sun seeing who could burst the most of these bubbles with their thumbs. But nowadays, he and Reggie had more important things to occupy their time. But some of the others, the ones who got pocket money off their dads every week and didn't have to earn their own, still sat in the street doing it all day.

After pulling their loads around the entry to his back yard, Sheridan went down the cellar to fetch a small hatchet. It was as sharp as a knife, so it didn't take long to get the ugly mass of wood transformed into an enormous pile of neat little chips. This task completed, they then began making small bundles of firewood, but to their annoyance, the flimsy string they were using kept snapping, until they decided to double it up.

When they eventually managed to get all the wood into secure bundles, Sheridan began loading Reggie's outstretched arms, before setting off on their first trip to the big posh houses in Chatham Street and Abercromby Square.

When this had been sold, they returned for a second load, which Reggie piled on to Sheridan's outstretched arms, before making off to Canning Street. They alternated like this for every trip until all the bundles had been sold. It was hard work, up and down the stairs of those huge old Georgian houses, then returning to the backyard for another load. But it was worth it. Before they finished, they'd sold ten shillings' worth, at threepence a bundle.

The weather being so warm, it took longer than usual to sell the firewood, and even then, they didn't sell it all. But they were happy enough to have their Hopey money and the price of some Williamson's Toffee and an "icey" when they got inside.

There was a James Stewart cowboy film showing tonight called *Winchester 73*, and, according to Thomas, you couldn't afford to miss it. Like Thomas, Sheridan loved cowboy films, especially those in Technicolor, because until recently he'd only ever seen Hopalong Cassidy or Roy Rogers or Gene Autrey at the Saturday Matinee, and they were never in colour.

Before they departed at teatime, Sheridan said he would call for his friend at six o'clock. The First House at the Hopey didn't start till half-six, but it would take them a while to get somebody to take them in, because they wouldn't let kids in of a night unless they were with a grown-up.

In the kitchen, Sheridan's Dad was sitting in the armchair still wearing his jacket and shirt and tie. His hair was neatly brushed back, and he looked a lot smarter than this morning.

Even when he had no money - which was most of the time - his Dad always got a shave and wore a clean white shirt and tie before going out. He always said that by looking clean and smart, he stood more chance of being taken in the pub by one of his many acquaintances than if he was scruffy, because when you were scruffy nobody wanted to know you. He'd discovered that, he said, through going out one night, after a heavy bout of drinking in the afternoon, wearing the same shirt he'd had on for days and not bothering to shave, and had ended up not getting a single pint off anyone. After that, he said, he regarded a clean shirt and shave as a kind of investment.

"Hello, son!" he greeted in a friendly manner. "Where've yer been?" It was as if the Gasman incident of this morning had never happened. He was just about drunk, pleasant drunk, thought Sheridan. He had to be. Everything fitted. His eyes weren't watery and his face red, like when he was rotten drunk. And his face, although slightly red and swollen again, wasn't half as bad as last night. More talking and singing drunk, than fighting drunk. Anyway, he thought, he couldn't be all that far gone because, for a start, his hair was still neatly in place. Sheridan reckoned he would be well sobered up by six o'clock at the latest. He'd seen him drunker than this of an afternoon and, after a cold swill, still be sober for half-five in time for the pubs opening. His Dad could really take his ale, he thought proudly.

"Been down the market", he replied. "we got some wood and loads of fades as well."

Pulling a crumpled Woodbine out of his top pocket, his Dad said, "Oh aye. Good on yer son. Nice to see yer getting by for yerself." Then, lighting the cigarette with a scrap of newspaper from the gas cooker, he went on, "I was a little progger when I was your age. Like to see that in a kid. Does no harm to rough it a bit."

The deep drag he took on the cigarette forced him to pause, before continuing, "God blimey, I roughed it when I was a kid. Begging bread with no shoes on, we were. There was no Dole or N.A.B. in them days. If yer didn't get out and about, yer fuckin' starved. Don't know how lucky they are these days."

It must have been terrible in those days, thought Sheridan. Yet, because it was an age he'd never known, it somehow seemed a more pleasant and adventurous time to have lived.

Settling once again in the armchair, his Dad asked him where his Mam was. Without knowing why, he immediately replied that she'd gone to the Co-op butcher's shop around the corner. But in truth, he didn't know where she was. Seemingly satisfied with the reply, his Dad, with a thoughtful look, hunched himself up in the sagging chair and began searching in his trouser pocket.

When he looked prosperously drunk like this, he would sometimes get carried away and give Sheridan as much as a two-shilling piece. So hearing the tinkle of coins in his pocket, he felt a pleasant thrill of expectation. But to his dismay, he merely handed him a shilling and told him to run and get the "Final" *'Echo*. This left him feeling disappointed and irritated. Why did he have to tell him to run? Why did he have to say that? Everyone knew he always ran on every errand he was sent.

Returning with the newspaper, he saw his Dad with a big plateful of cow's tripe in front of him, cut into small pieces. Saturating every piece with loads of vinegar and salt, he began eating it with his fingers. It sickened Sheridan just to look at it. But the way he went through the actions of eating; chewing, smacking his lips and everything, made anything he ate seem so delicious.

Picking up one of the larger pieces, his Dad said, "Here yer are, are yer having a taste?" But, grimacing with disgust, he shook his head.

"Don't know what's good for yiz, yer don't", he said, popping the tripe into his own mouth.

"Dad, they didn't have the Final." said Sheridan handing him the *'Echo*. "It's not up yet. So I had to get the Half-Time."

"Don't worry about it lad, that'll do fine", he replied.

When he was sober on weekdays, he always insisted on the "Final Edition" of the *'Echo*, in order to get the very latest racing results and the most up to date stop press news. And if Sheridan brought back an earlier edition, he would make him take it straight back. When he'd been drinking though, he wasn't bothered about what edition he got.

Handing him back the tenpence change, his Dad said absently, "Yer can have that, son."

Oh! he thought, it was certainly his day all right! Another tenpence now on top of the firewood money. It seemed as if money was coming in from everywhere! It was like that dream he was always having, where there were tanners and shillings and half-crowns all over the pavement and in the gutter. And as he kept picking them up and stuffing them into his already bulging pockets, there was always more of them, and then more and more. The only thing about that dream though, he thought, was that it didn't half make you feel lousy and disappointed when you woke up. Sometimes though, it was so real he would jump out of bed and start searching through his pockets, but there was never even so much as a farthing, never mind half-dollars. How could there be? All his pockets had holes in them.

Now glancing through the *'Echo*, his Dad seemed to have had enough of the tripe, but was still trying with his tongue to remove the last remnants from between his teeth. You could tell he'd really enjoyed it.

Feeling loaded, and full of gratitude towards his Dad, he asked, "D'yer want a cup of tea?"

"No yer alright", he replied, "I'm aces." Then suddenly he asked, "Where's the other fella? At the stupid football match again?"

His manner wasn't angry, but Sheridan knew how much he hated football. "Twenty-two lunatics kicking a ball of wind around", he called it. He always said football was why all the people were always so thick.

"I don't know, Dad", he replied. Then trying to cover up for Thomas in case he was at the match, "But I don't think so. I think he's working overtime this afternoon."

"Overtime?" he said mockingly, "What the bleedin'ell's he working overtime for? He's only on boy's money anyway. Never any better off, the stupid cunt." Then, as if it had just occurred to him, he added, "Never gives me fuck all."

Sheridan knew Thomas had been drinking ever since he'd left school, and that on Saturday afternoons, he usually had a few pints straight after work, before going to the match. But he daren't tell his Dad. He would be as mad as hell if he'd known that. He wouldn't have minded Thomas drinking. He would have actually welcomed that. That would have been a sign of his manliness to his Dad. But to drink on the sly, when he could be drinking openly with his own father? To him that would have been disloyalty, perhaps even treachery. He wouldn't be able to see that Thomas just wanted to mix with his own mates, and that young fellas these days didn't drink with their dads like they did years ago. But that would have made no difference. He'd still regard Thomas as a tight-fisted traitor to his own family. And if he knew about him going to the match as well, to watch the lunatics, that would really have driven him crazy.

Sheridan remembered only too well the many late nights he'd keep Thomas and himself up, talking to them about football and the government and religion and things. There was one Saturday night in particular, he recalled, when what he'd said made him really think about it. He'd been telling them about the way things were when he was a kid and about how they were always poverty-stricken and hungry all the time. "D'yiz know what", he'd said, "the only difference between you'se and me when I was a kid, is that we were kept down by the Catholic religion and you'se are all being kept down by football." Thomas had got a bit brave that night, because he'd had a few pints, and said it was only a harmless game and that, if millions of people enjoyed it, what was wrong with that? Sheridan had silently agreed with him and both of them had thought their Dad was a miserable spoilsport. But, responding angrily to this challenge from Thomas, his Dad had shouted, "Listen you, yer stupid bastard, I'm a lot older than you! I'm fuckin' telling yer. Listen to yer father!" It seemed he was desperate to be understood, as he went on, "When millions of people are safely locked inside football grounds every fuckin' Saturday shouting their fuckin' heads off over nothing, you'll never get a revolution or anything like that. Yer government, yer lords, yer aristocracy, they're not fuckin' stupid, they all know that. They're laughing their fuckin' heads off at you stupid bastards. Keep the mugs happy, they're saying to each other, while they're pissing on yiz."

The more he spoke, the more excited he'd seemed to become as he went on, "Just like we were kept ignorant and in poverty by the priests and confession and the catechism and all that palaver", he went on, "you'se are the same with the fuckin' football mania."

The intensity of this outburst had jolted Thomas into showing some interest. Sheridan too had begun to pay more attention, partly through fear, but also because it was interesting.

His Dad had become really agitated that night and had given him a fright when he suddenly sprang from the chair, as if to give himself more authority. He was sure he was going to hit Thomas, but instead, his tone unexpectedly became quieter yet still determined.

"Listen", he'd said, "why d'yiz think a country like Germany, which was on her knees and bankrupt ten years before the war, could take on practically the whole world? I'll tell yer why shall I? Why she had us fucked for a start? Because in the Twenties and Thirties, when everyone in this country was kept docile and ignorant every week at football matches, the Germans were being politically educated at rallies, and being trained in physical fitness and being taught to be manly and have pride in themselves. They were told all the while they were the best. Hitler made them alert and hard and proud. 'Guns before butter', he used to shout and they loved him. He had the right idea, he kept them discontented because he knew people are fuckin' useless when they're too contented."

It had made him very nervous. It always did when his Dad got worked up like that. But eventually he'd sat down. Then, after a few moments pause, he'd asked in a strange quizzical way, "What's the only difference between a herd of stampeding cattle and the crowd at a football match when a goal's scored?" Sheridan had shook his head and Thomas had said in a faintly cheeky way, "I don't know. Tell us?"

Taking a deep drag of the soggy roll-up, which had caused his eyes to squint in a sinister fashion, he'd replied, "The cattle all cry 'Moo, Moo' and the crowd all shout 'Goal! Goal!' That's the only fuckin' difference. That's why yer always wanna be yer own man. Always be a performer, don't be a spectator. Never be just one of the fuckin' crowd, because that's all you'll ever be, a number, a unit, just part of a mindless fuckin' herd."

Despite the tense atmosphere and his stern tone, the way he'd said "Moo, Moo" had made Sheridan burst out laughing. But when he'd saw him glaring at Thomas, he quickly stopped.

After that night, he realised just how much his Dad hated football. But Thomas never seemed to realise it. Or, he thought, maybe he was just being defiant. But, as for himself, even before that night, it didn't bother him much. He wasn't interested in football. He'd much rather be down the market or climbing on the garage roofs or sitting in the Hopey on a Saturday afternoon.

His Dad was now intently reading the 'Echo, as if to digest as much of it as possible before going back out on the ale. He still hadn't taken his jacket off, so that meant he had no intention of staying in. But, thought Sheridan, he'd never stay in anyway, not once he'd tasted the ale in the afternoon - especially a Saturday afternoon. He'd often heard him saying how terrible the feeling was when you'd had a good bevy in the afternoon and couldn't get a "livener" in the evening. The ale, he would say, dies in you and makes you feel terrible all night because you're neither sober nor drunk.

Putting the kettle on, he began carving himself a thick crust off the fresh farmhouse loaf from the coal cupboard. It was ages, he thought, since he'd been able to get the "knocker", the fresh crust, because Thomas always and ever claimed it - even if there was another loaf already broken into.

Finding the butter dish empty, he searched everywhere for the margarine, but there wasn't any. There wasn't even any planted. There was some syrup left in a tin though. He'd been really looking forward to the thick fresh crust smothered with margarine and syrup, but syrup wasn't much good on its own. So grabbing a cup of "dripping" off the shelf over the cooker, he plastered the crust with that instead. He loved dripping butties, especially with plenty of salt on. This wasn't real beef or pork dripping though, only kipper's fat. He didn't miss the taste of real dripping anyway, because they hardly ever had it in their house. It was too dear.

As he sweetened his tea with a spoonful of "Conny-onny" from the condensed milk tin, his Dad, with a look of amusement, called him over. There was something in the *'Echo* he wanted to show him.

He would often point things out in the paper to him. Sheridan knew he was kind of proud of him through being able to read since he was six. And it was very flattering the way he'd ask him to read things out of the paper, as if to say, "What is your opinion about that?" Or, "I know you will twig the humour or the sadness or whatever in that." To be treated with such respect by his Dad made him feel really important - even if he didn't understand half of the things pointed out to him.

"Read that", said his Dad, as if confident he would immediately grasp its meaning. Sheridan looked to where his finger rested on the page. It said, "Today's Quotation" and he began reading quickly, because he didn't want to seem disrespectful by making his Dad wait after he had been so respectful to him.

"Not many sounds in life,
and I include all urban and rural sounds,
exceeds in interest a knock at the door
- Charles Lamb."

The words recalled the miserable memory of this morning. "What does that remind yer of?" asked his Dad with a grin. "The Gasman", he immediately replied.

Clapping his hands, his Dad cried out with delight, "Got it! It's true what they say alright... great minds think alike!"

It seemed obvious to Sheridan. But he still felt really flattered, even though he didn't really know what "urban" or "rural" meant. "I bet that gink never had a creditor knocking on his door in his life", said his Dad. "Bet he never even had a knocker", said Sheridan ruefully.

Chapter Six

They waited for ages outside the Hopey asking people to take them in, until finally a man and woman obliged them. But as they approached the paybox, the man asked what price seats they were going in. "The Tenpennies", said Sheridan, hoping that the man and woman were too. But handing back the money, the man casually said, "Oh here lad, here's yer money. We're going upstairs in the One and Threes." As they sneaked back outside, unsure of whether Old Alf, the doorman had seen them, the woman gave them a pitying backward glance.

"The doorman's seen us now", said Reggie. "We're fucked! Might as well go up to the Cappy now." Sheridan ignored him, not only because the *Capitol* was miles away up a steep hill, but also because he didn't like swearing in public. But somehow, he was always envious at the grown-up way Reggie always swore. It seemed to make him so much better than himself.

"The bastard", he swore, trying to equal Reggie, "You'd think he'd have told us in the first place he was going in the One and Threes. If the doorman's seen us, we've had it now." He was really angry with the man and woman for raising their hopes after getting so many refusals. Trying to discover where they'd gone wrong. Reggie asked, "What did yer say to him?"

"I just gave him the half-a-dollar and asked him to take two in."

"Well, that's it then. He's thought we were going in the one and threes. Two One and Threes make half a crown. Yer should have said, 'take two Tenpennies in'." As well as his swearing, his friend seemed even more superior to him now by exposing his silly mistake. He really felt stupid, especially, because in school he was a lot cleverer than Reggie.

As they talked under the shabby picture house canopy, it began raining as the scruffy doorman appeared on the entrance steps, peering up and down the street. Old Alf, who was about seventy-five, had been the Hopey's doorman for as long as anyone could remember. The grown-up regulars always called him Admiral Benbow, on account of the numerous medals he wore on his sky-blue oversized scruffy tunic, which was full of beer stains and cigarette ash. But although the grown-ups were amused by his appearance – especially the baggy trousers, which didn't match his tunic and the dirty grey plimsolls he always wore, he was nevertheless very strict about underage kids trying to get in of a night time.

Diving into one of the exit doorways, the two friends stood frozen, their backs to the door, hardly daring to breathe. And because it was so quiet and deserted, they could clearly hear the magical sounds of gunshots and dramatic music coming from inside. "Aw fuckin'ell", whispered Reggie, "the Big Picture's started. We're gonna miss half of it." He sounded really upset and didn't seem to realize that this was only the First House, and that they'd have a chance to see the whole picture later on in the Second House. He wasn't so clever and grown-up after all, thought Sheridan. And after explaining this to him, he felt he'd evened up the score with him.

After several minutes, Reggie, his back still glued to the door, said, "Have a look to see if Old Alf's gone back in." The outside of the Hopey, although deserted, was brightly lit up as Sheridan peeped out. It was all clear. The rain had stopped and as Old Alf went back inside, there was a scruffy old man shuffling towards them. Adopting a pitiful expression, Sheridan pleaded, "Hey mister, can you take two in please?"

"What are yiz going in?" he asked with a suspicious look.

"The Tenpennies"

"Oh, alright. Giz yer money then."

Handing him the half-crown, Sheridan, although nervous and excited, felt like singing and shouting with sheer happiness. Their long wait was over. At last, they were going in!

"Aw thanks, mister", he said, desperately hoping he wouldn't change his mind at the last minute like the couple earlier on.

Unsure of whether they'd been spotted earlier by Old Alf, they kept themselves well tucked in behind the old man as they approached the paybox. But he took so long fumbling in his pockets for his own money, that the doorman was beginning to scrutinise them. The suspense was so unbearable that Reggie whispered, "Come on you old bastard. Fuckin' hurry up!" And despite trying to look unworried, Sheridan's stomach was turning over. The old man was maddening. Why didn't he put a bleedin' move on?! At last, he said to the woman in the small hatch that was the paybox, "Three Tenpennies, missus." Then seeing the tickets actually in the old man's hand, Sheridan was so relieved he felt like thumbing his nose at Old Alf. But, realising they weren't actually inside yet, he thought better about it.

As they trod cautiously behind the old man, trying to be as inconspicuous as possible, Alf suddenly pounced.

"Hey, how old are you?" he shouted. They both turned and asked, "Who? Me?"

"You!" he demanded, pointing at Sheridan. This is it, he thought with a sinking feeling, his exhilaration rapidly fading. But trying to hide his fright and disappointment he went on the attack. "Me?" he said indignantly, "I'm nearly fifteen."

"When was yer born then?" demanded Alf.

He felt more confident now, because he'd worked it all out in case he was ever asked this question. "Fourth of July, Nineteen Thirty-Six", he replied. "Oh, go on then", said the doorman, as if he couldn't be bothered anymore.

As they walked through the foyer, past the four large coloured photos of Errol Flynn. Humphrey Bogart, Joan Crawford and Bette Davis, the old man, who seemed a bit deaf, muttered, "What was *he* on about lad?"

"Oh," he casually replied, "he just didn't believe how old I am."

"*He* doesn't believe?" he cried. "Who the bleedin'ell is he not to believe anybody! *He's* the biggest liar on two fuckin' feet. Been on the N.A.B for years, he has. Down there every week, he is, crying poverty while he's working here every night, cash in hand. Cheeky bastard." The old man seemed to be really jealous of Alf, as he went on, "Good job they don't know about the cheeky bastard working when he's on the fuckin' King Cole! Yer can go to jail for fiddling the N.A.B, yer know."

"Is that right, mister?" said Sheridan, the value of this information hitting him immediately. But he wasn't going to let anyone else in on it. Not even Reggie. *He* might tell his mam and dad and they'd spoil the whole thing, because they were real law-abiding and might tell the police and Alf might be sacked. Reggie's dad was never out of work, and he'd shop anyone he knew who was working and getting Dole or the N.A.B. at the same time. As for his own Dad, *he* admired anyone who could get away with something like that. And so did he. Nevertheless, if what the old man had told him about Old Alf was true, he'd never again have any trouble getting in the Hopey at night - even if the picture was a certificate X - now that he knew the doorman's weak spot. Already happy at being able to get in, knowing this made him feel even happier.

Once inside in the dark, Reggie began tugging Sheridan's jersey from behind. "Hey, we're not sitting with *him*", he whispered behind the old man's back "I know", he whispered back, "but he's still got our *change*."

The old man handed their tickets in to Old Lizzie, who had worked there for years and was also the ice cream seller. But because there were no *real* usherettes in the Hopey, and Lizzie had no torch, they had to feel their own way in the darkness to their seats in the front. Once out of earshot of Lizzie, the old man slipped the change to Sheridan and whispered mischievously, "Go on lads, you'se can go your own way now." He seemed to have got a big kick out of the three of them fooling the doorman.

Feeling the shilling coin in the darkness, Sheridan didn't need any light. He could feel the edges, so he knew the old man hadn't cheated him.

As the two friends grew accustomed to the darkness, they spotted the old man cheekily working his way along a row of seats in the One and Sixes. Sheridan was glad for him and thought he deserved a comfortable seat for taking them in. Only for him they could have been standing outside all night. But

Reggie just laughed and said, "Look at the old fella. Cheeky fucker, isn't he?"

It was great in the Hopey on a Saturday night. The place was packed out. Even the One and Threes in the "circle" upstairs, but down the two sides, the wooden benches weren't as full.

The Tenpennies downstairs, also wooden benches, which must have been pews back when it was a chapel, were the nearest to the screen and they were packed. There were mostly big lads of seventeen and eighteen upstairs in the pews, who had bunked in. After they'd seen the full programme in the First House, these lads would start messing around and would have everyone distracted and laughing at the antics they got up to.

Sheridan and Reggie managed to squeeze into the third row of the Tenpennies from the front. Although the benches were hard and uncomfortable and your neck ached from looking up at the screen, you could at least *hear* what was being said. Not like the Saturday Matinee, thought Sheridan. It was terrible then. You couldn't hear a thing through all the kids shouting and screaming "Boo!" every time a "baddie" cowboy appeared, and yelling "Hooray!" whenever Roy Rogers or Hopalong Cassidy or The Lone Ranger rode into view. He felt really grown-up to be in here on a Saturday night. The smell of oranges and sweets and cigarette smoke was everywhere, and nearly everyone was a grown-up. It felt great just to be part of it. The only other time he'd felt like this, was when there had been torchlight parades around Abercromby Square and all over the city, and he'd been allowed to stay up late and mix with all kinds of grown-ups. That was when the war had ended, and Brendan had carried him on his shoulders to watch the torchlight parades.

It must be about the best thing in the world to be grown-up, he thought. But being in here now was the next best thing. He'd only ever been in here once at night, but never on a Saturday night. There was nothing to touch the Hopey for atmosphere on a Saturday night; no place on earth like it. He felt so special and privileged and full of awe just sitting there.

They hadn't been in long, when the Big Picture ended and the lights came on. Sheridan was glad they'd only seen a little bit, there would be that much more to see in the Second House. But Reggie was annoyed, because they'd now seen the ending. He said that only for Old Alf the doorman, he would have waited in the foyer for it to finish, like some grown-ups did, so as not to spoil the ending later.

It was like some hectic marketplace now, with big lads and girls shouting across the rows of benches to each other, and walking around the auditorium, and jumping over the benches to be with their newly spotted friends. And upstairs, the big lads were whistling down to other lads and girls in the Tenpennies, and throwing dog-ends and orange peel and empty ice cream cartons. Most of these, who had bunked in through the back door without paying, were from the Bullring tenements. They weren't scared of Old Alf or Lizzie or even the Manager or anyone, so nobody ever went near them. The only time they quietened down was when a sergeant and a constable regularly came in near the end of the Second House and stood at the back. But by that time, most of them had left anyhow.

The people in the comfortable One and Six seats at the back thought they were posh and looked down on those in the Tenpennies. They were mostly men like Reggie's dad and mam, or were older people like the man who had taken them in earlier. Annoyed at the chaotic atmosphere, some of these began shouting things like, "Why don't yiz bleedin' well shut up!" and, "Let's hear something will yiz!" But nobody took any notice of them. To Sheridan, they seemed a shower of miserable spoilsports, because, when the lights were on, the screen was blank, so there was nothing to hear anyway. He guessed they were just showing off because they were in the poshest seats.

At long last the Second House began, and as the lights went down, the *Gaumont British News* came on, then the trailer for next Monday, Tuesday and Wednesday's programme. It was for *The Jolson Story* and Sheridan was mesmerised throughout. He decided that if he never saw another film in his whole life, he was definitely going to see this. And even though he feared that seeing it would probably shatter most of his illusions about his Dad and his singing - like reading the proper words of the poems had done - he knew he just *had* to see it. When the trailer ended, Reggie said, "I'm gonna see that Sheh, are you?"

"Yeah." His reply was deceptively casual, but, he thought, if only he knew just how determined I am to see it.

When they saw the trailers for any film, declaring they were going to see it was a way of appearing to be more sophisticated and being confident of acquiring enough picture money and of being taken in. But in truth, they hardly ever managed to see the picture. This time though, Sheridan was utterly determined. He was going to see *The Jolson Story* if it killed him! And what made him so confident was the secret realisation that, so long as he could get his picture money, he would have no trouble getting in - not with what he now knew about Old Alf being on the Dole and working at the same time!

After the trailer ended, the words "Full Supporting Programme" appeared on the screen and Reggie said, "That picture's always on. Wonder what it's about?"

"What picture?" asked a puzzled Sheridan. "That one, 'Full Supporting Programme'", he said, pointing at the screen. This caused him to suddenly burst out laughing. Until now he had been feeling uneasy with Reggie. All night he'd seemed to be showing him up, making him feel less clever than him. He wasn't doing it deliberately, he thought. It was just a way he had about him. But it had been troubling him. For a start, there was the bad language he seemed to use so easily, with such confidence. Then there was the telling off for not asking the man and woman to take them in the Tenpennies. Then on top of that, there was Old Alf pulling him up rather than Reggie, about his age. That had really angered him: the grown-up way Reggie had just strode ahead with the old man, leaving him feeling like a stupid little kid at the mercy of the doorman. And what really exasperated him about all of this was that, apart from being cleverer than Reggie, he was also two months older. But now, he thought, Reggie's stupidity had brought everything back to what it should be. They were equal once again, with him feeling just a little more equal than his friend.

"Yer soft bleeder", he scoffed. "*that's* not a picture. That means the trailer and the news and everything." Looking sheepish, Reggie was silent as Sheridan again began laughing. "It's always on", he mimicked, mocking Reggie. But his laughter at his friend's discomfort was short-lived, as a deafening voice suddenly bellowed in his ear from the row behind, "Hey you big mouth, shut yer fuckin' trap!"

His ears tickling with the roaring sound, he turned to see a big, fat, ugly face topped with a mop of black unruly hair staring hatefully into him. The face looked enormous. Its owner must have been at least eighteen, he thought. "You fuckin' heard what I said!" the face roared again. He knew he couldn't argue with such a frightening animal. Now it was Reggie's turn to laugh. But his laughter didn't last long either. "And *you!*" roared the face again. Sheridan decided that as soon as the place thinned out, they would move away. He'd never be able to enjoy the Big Picture with this hateful baboon breathing down his neck. He hated hatred. He'd seen enough of it between his Mam and Dad. And that's what was on this brute's face – pure, ignorant hatred. Feeling completely powerless, he whispered to Reggie, "I'd like to see him do that if our kid was here."

"Yeah", he whispered back, "your Thomas would fuckin' kill him."

Suddenly he felt proud that someone, especially someone like Reggie, someone outside of his own family, respected his brother's fighting ability so much. But the thought of Thomas also made him feel sad that *he* never came here anymore. This made him yearn for the day when he too, like his brother, would be able to go downtown to the likes of the *Forum,* the *Futurist* and the *Palais-de-Luxe*, without having to beg anyone to take him in, and without big lads telling you to shut your fuckin' trap.

They had been saving for the Big Picture their bars of Williamson's toffee, bought under the counter, from McDonough's sweet shop. So as soon as it started, Sheridan pulled his out. It had gone quite soft through being in his back trouser pocket. Hearing the rustling sound of the toffee paper in the dark, Reggie asked, "Are you eating yours now?"

"Yeah, why not? Big Picture's started, hasn't it?"

Reggie's bar was harder, so he tried to break off the squares on the back of the bench, but it was too hard. He was making so much noise trying to break the toffee that Ugly Face called him a little cunt and told him to, "make less fuckin' noise." Because of this he frantically dashed out to the foyer. Frustrated because, this being the Second House, he would never be able to see again the part of the film he'd missed, he quickly smashed the toffee bar into pieces on the marble steps to Upstairs and dashed back. When he asked what had happened in his absence, there was no reply from Sheridan, who was engrossed in the film.

The toffee seemed to make *Winchester 73* even more enjoyable. After finishing it all off, they were both as thirsty as hell, so Sheridan offered his friend the money to get two ice-cream cups off Old Lizzie. But Reggie, because he'd already missed enough of the picture, said, "Aw, you go and get them, Sheh." But pointing out that he had paid the old man to take them in here in the first place, Sheridan refused. Annoyed at this, Reggie protested, "I've already missed some of the picture." But then quickly realising Sheridan was paying for them, he agreed to go. He could be a crafty bugger when he wanted to be, thought Sheridan. And he didn't like people who took advantage of other people - especially if they were supposed to be friends.

Everyone who went to the Hopey knew Old Lizzie, even the kids at the Saturday Matinee. She'd worked there for years and years. Everyone said she was a bit soft in the head, because she had a big hump on her back and always wore a pair of men's socks for gloves when serving the ice creams and lolly ices. Some people also called her "Mary Killed The Cat", because of a rumour that she kept lots of cats and occasionally killed some of them to make soup with. She also had an odd habit of walking backwards along the aisles, shouting, "Ice Cream, Ice Cream", along every single row. Even when she would reach the front of the Tenpennies, she would still walk backwards, underneath the screen, across to the other aisle. Everybody would call her all kinds of names and shout insults at her, and people, especially those in the One and Sixes, were always shouting at her to "shut up" and be quiet so that they could hear the picture. But she never took any notice of anyone.

Although she was facing Reggie as she walked backwards, he had to shout, "Hey Lizzie!" several times, before she finally stopped. "What d'yer want?" she murmured suspiciously. As the little light from the tray shone up into her squinting, sheep-like eyes, it gave her a witch-like expression. "Two cups, Lizzie", he replied.

As she was serving Reggie, a gang of big lads appeared from nowhere and surrounded her. They were making a terrible noise, all shouting at the same time for different things, until she shouted back at them, "Alright! Alright! Hold yer fuckin' horses. I've only got one pair of fuckin' hands!" Amid the chaos and confusion, Reggie saw several hands helping themselves from the tray, cheekily stealing ice cream cups and lolly ices, but Lizzie didn't seem to notice. Suddenly there was loud whistling and jeering from the benches upstairs. Someone shouted, "Now Lizzie, have yer pissed yer drawers yet?" Everybody started laughing and orange peel and empty ice-cream cups came showering down all around her, some of them hitting her on the head. Some big brawny man, who looked like a docker, sitting in the One and Sixes with his fat wife and trying to look respectable, shouted out, "Let's fuckin' well hear something will yiz!" You could hardly hear the picture now for all the shouting and jeering and whistling, when another voice from the darkness upstairs shouted back down to the docker, "Got a crush on Mary Killed The Cat, have yer, Grandad?" Then somebody else shouted, "He's only after his fuckin' sweaty socks back off Lizzie!" and widespread laughter broke out once more.

When Reggie got back with the ice creams, he found Sheridan, like everybody else in the front rows, standing up on the bench to see what was going on with Lizzie. By now everyone seemed to have forgotten about the picture.

"What's up?" he asked excitedly. "I don't know", replied Reggie, "but all them big fellas are robbing Old Lizzie blind. They're robbing all the iceys and everything."

Sitting back down, amid all the commotion, they found it hard to follow the picture. Handing him a cup, Reggie said, "I wish they'd all shut up. I wanna see the rest of the fuckin' picture. I've missed loads already!"

"Yeah, so do I", he replied. "It's worse than the Saturday Matinee, this."

It had taken the Hopey Manager to put all the lights on and, standing beneath the screen with a big stick in his hand, threaten to stop the film, before everybody finally quietened down. But no sooner had the situation returned to normal, than the picture broke down, with big numbers racing up and down the screen. This prompted more rowdy commotion with everybody shouting once again amid raucous laughter. "Put a fuckin' shillin' in the meter!" shouted one voice. And, "Lizzie's done the fuckin' Lecky meter again!" cried out another. But whatever the fault was, it was fixed very quickly and the picture started again. But even then, there were people grumbling and saying that it had only been an excuse to cut the picture to bits. And Sheridan wondered how grown-up people always knew when a picture had been cut, because he could never tell.

As *Winchester 73* neared its end, many people had by now left and the Hopey seemed to feel much colder and sadder. There were now numerous empty spaces along the Tenpenny benches and dozens of empty seats in the One and Sixes. And upstairs, the benches that ran along both sides of the auditorium were practically deserted. It seemed to Sheridan a completely different place from the loud, lively place of a few hours ago, an altogether sadder place. And knowing he and Reggie would also soon be leaving, making him even sadder, he suddenly felt a sickly churning in his stomach. He'd completely forgotten that he had to be home by ten o'clock, not only that, it was Saturday night! As there was no clock in here like in other picture houses, he really started to panic, but he did his best to hide it from Reggie.

Worried to death about not being in the house to greet them, he would feel a lot easier if he were already there listening to them coming up the street. He would feel in charge then. If he were already in the house when they came home, there were many things he could do to stave off the fighting - at least till Thomas came in. He could pour out their ale. Or he could make them a cup of tea and a sandwich to sober them up a bit. Or he could humour them. Or, if the worst came to the worst, he could even sing a happy song to distract them. But the thought of *not* being there when they came home filled him with aching guilt. Thomas wouldn't even be home till about eleven, he thought, because he usually hung around outside the Chippy with other lads and girls when he came home from the pictures of a Saturday night.

Suddenly, another heavier pain hit him mercilessly in the pit of his stomach. If there was nobody in the house when his Mam and Dad got home, how were they going to get in?! And if they couldn't get in, that's when the *real* murder would start. His Dad had no patience at all when he was drunk. If he got mad through not being able to get in, he would start roaring his head off and making a show of the family. His imagination was now racing out of control. Vivid images filled his head of his Dad beating hell out of his Mam, with crowds of smug, curious people, who never did that sort of thing themselves, watching their shame. Reggie's dad would certainly be one of them, he thought.

"Hey, mister", he shouted to a man a few rows back, "have yer got the time on yer?" The man seemed to take an eternity to pull out an old fob watch from his waistcoat pocket. "Hurry up yer old bastard", he muttered to himself.

"Just five to ten son." Sorry for calling him an old bastard, Sheridan felt like hugging the man. He could just as easily have said ten o'clock, or even ten past or half past ten! Luck was really on his side, he thought, as he glanced at the screen and realised that this was where they had come in, so he wouldn't even have to miss any of the picture. More importantly, he wouldn't have to shame himself to Reggie by saying he *had* to leave to be home for ten. He could truthfully say he was leaving because they'd now seen what they'd missed in the First House.

Nudging his friend, he said, "This is where we came in. Come on, are yer coming?"

"Ah hey," he replied sleepily. "There's not much left. We might as well watch it to the end now."

What was he to do now? He knew the pubs stopped serving at ten-to-ten. For all he knew his Mam and Dad might be so drunk that they were already making their way home. It was all right for Reggie, he thought enviously, *his* mam and dad didn't even drink. He would have loved to have been in his shoes. He must never have known what it was like to be scared or worried in his life.

With time passing quickly Sheridan knew, if Reggie wasn't going to leave with him, he had to act fast.

"Won't be a minute", he said, trying to sound as casual as possible, "I'm just going the lav."

"Aw hang on a minute", said Reggie grudgingly, "it'll be the end in a few minutes. But Sheridan was becoming more exasperated. How would he like to be suffering like this, he thought. It would've been lovely to have been Reggie right now, the lucky bastard. Why did he have to be so awkward?

"Ah, I can't hold on any longer. I'm pissing myself", he cried desperately, hoping his friend didn't suspect anything. Then without saying anything further, he raced along the aisle, out into the deserted street and ran as fast as he could all the way home.

Amazingly, he only tripped over once. But even as he tucked the nuisance of a stocking back inside the flapping toecap of his boot, he was more worried about how he was going to explain himself to Reggie tomorrow. But he finally decided, "Oh fuck him. I'll tell him I had a shit instead and couldn't find him when I came back."

Chapter Seven

Approaching their street, Sheridan saw a crowd of people outside the pub on the corner. Some were singing, others simply standing about talking. Nervously searching the faces of them all, he couldn't find his Mam's or Dad's. That made him feel better. They weren't here. They couldn't be inside the pub, because it was now closed. And, as they weren't fighting in the street, he reckoned they must be in another pub... or at least on their way home. One thing he was sure of and glad about, they weren't home yet, and that made him feel even better. As the dread gradually faded away, he stopped running now and leisurely strolled the rest of the way down their street.

Knowing it would be futile knocking on the front door, he went around the back entry. His aim was to climb over the wall into the yard, then go down the stone steps and through the cellar, which was always open because there was no door on it.

It was dark up the entry. It shouldn't have been really, because the Corporation workmen had only recently erected a big gas lamp high up at the corner of the entry, but someone had smashed it with stones. Everybody had blamed the kids in the street, but he was sure he would've known if it had been one of them.

The bricks and mortar of the backyard walls were really old and rotten and there were gaps between the bricks, where the mortar had decayed and fallen away. But this made it easy to climb the walls. He had become one of the best climbers in the neighbourhood through practising on these walls. He could practically run up the walls of the nearby bombed houses, as fast as the big tom cats ran up the telegraph pole in their street.

With the backyard door locked, he was feeling in the dark for a suitable gap in the bricks to start his climb, when suddenly he heard loud, heavy breathing. It felt strange, this sound, and there was a strong warm smell of perfume. But strangely, instead of being scared, he felt curious and kind of excited. He seemed to sense there was no danger in this situation; that whoever was there, was there for their own reasons and weren't any threat to him.

Suddenly he heard the sound of shuffling feet and the rustling of clothes. Then amid the smell of its smoke, he saw the red glow of a cigarette flaring up then going dull. Becoming gradually used to the darkness, he noticed the outline of a woman's form leaning with her back to the wall a few yards down the entry. The heavy rasping sound had now died down, as he made out the hazy figure of a big man in an overcoat facing the woman.

The man was leaning with one arm against the wall over the woman's shoulder, as if he was questioning her, and both were murmuring almost in whispers to each other. He couldn't make out what they were saying, but he knew why they were there. And he knew what they had been doing. The woman, he was certain, was a prostitute. His Dad had told him and Thomas all about dirty women like her. Not only that, he'd sometimes even seen them himself, in the light summer nights, going down the entry with men.

One night last summer, when dusk was falling, he and Reggie had seen one going down the entry with a scruffy, red-faced man dressed in working clothes, and they had gone into his backyard and climbed on the wall to watch. What they saw didn't make him feel disgusted though, the way his Dad had said it would. Instead, it gave him a sort of weird feeling he'd never felt before. It had a kind of private warm atmosphere. It had excited him, and when the man's breathing had got louder and faster, making his body tremble and shake all over, he'd felt a sort of glow of pleasure sweep over him. He sensed that this was when the man shot into the woman; the time his Dad had told him about, when a baby is made. But prostitutes, he'd thought, must have been different from other women because, according to his Dad, *they* never had babies.

Still looking down from the wall, Sheridan watched as the two figures moved further up the entry. He was surprised that they hadn't said a word or chased him away. For a moment it occurred to him that they might even be afraid of *him*! And that they were trying to hide, because they were doing wrong. He couldn't believe it. Instead of chasing him away, it was they who were moving!

He wasn't sure whether they had already done it or whether they were waiting for him to leave first. But if they hadn't, that made him feel even more important: they were actually leaving because of him. There was another way out at the other end of the entry, so he guessed that maybe they were going to leave that way, but he couldn't be sure. He pondered about crawling along the backyard walls to watch them some more, but the sudden thought of his Mam and Dad forced him to quickly forget the idea.

Quickly climbing over the wall, he was in the backyard in no time. The yard was in darkness through the gaslight in the kitchen being out. The feeling of dread returned when he thought of having to go down the dank stone steps, green with slime, then all the way across the dark cellar and up into the unlit kitchen. As well as scary, it was maddening. Why the fuckin'ell couldn't they have "Lecky" like Reggie's and everyone else's house in the street, he suddenly thought.

The silence and darkness was overwhelming. It was pitch black everywhere, and he felt really scared now. But he knew it had to be done, and done quickly, before they came home. So, bracing himself, he began feeling his way down the slippery steps. Once in the cellar, he lost all sense of direction. It seemed he'd never be able to make his way across to the stairs, because there was no chink of light to guide him. Whistling in the dark, he suddenly felt faintly ashamed at himself, because he knew he was only whistling out of fear.

At last, he managed to get upstairs and into the kitchen. Seeing one of the gas rings on a low light, he lit a screwed up a piece of old newspaper, climbed onto the rickety table and lit the gas mantle with it. But as he tried to jump back down, he tripped and fell flat on his face. How stupid and selfish that Thomas was, he thought angrily. Okay, so maybe it doesn't go dark till about half-nine these nights, but knowing it would be dark when their Mam and Dad came in, he still should have lit the gas mantle before he'd gone out.

The kitchen, which was also the living room, was in a terrible state, with dirty dishes, unwashed plates and cups covering the table and dirty pans on the cooker. If his Mam and Dad saw the place like this, he thought, they would go crazy. So he frantically began tidying up as best he could, hiding the dirty pans in the cupboard.

One of the first things his Dad did when he became violent was tip up the table, sending dishes and plates flying everywhere. Not only that, he thought, but sauce bottles, butter dishes and sugar basins, especially heavy glass ones, could be very wicked weapons when thrown at someone in a temper. But the worst thing was the sound of breaking glass. He hated that. When his Dad would run amok with the poker, smashing all the cut glass mirrors in the big Victorian sideboard, the sound would terrify him. And why his Mam kept buying another secondhand sideboard, he'd never know, because sooner or later, his Dad always ended up wrecking them too. But he reckoned maybe there was a method in her madness: his Dad had often said that, if he didn't have something to smash, something to vent his anger on, he'd probably have battered her to death with the poker by now. So, he thought that perhaps the secondhand sideboards were a sort of insurance policy to his Mam.

He felt guilty about putting the dirty dishes into the bowl of already dirty, greasy water. But, he thought, I'm definitely not going back down in that cellar, with all the mice and slugs and everything down there - especially being on my own in the house at this time of night.

After clearing the table, he hid all the knives away and put the two glass vases off the sideboard into the coal cupboard. He then got out the almost hairless broom and gave the floor, which was littered with breadcrumbs and dog-ends, a quick brush.

Sweeping the dirt onto the hearth, he noticed the fireplace full of ashes, which had been there for days and it struck him how miserable it was these nights with the fire out all the time. Even though it was summer and warm and everything, it still felt sad to see the grate full of dead ashes and cinders, where there used to be a big roaring, homely fire. That was the only fault with summer, he thought. The fireplace was always dirty and lifeless and full of ashes, and the fire was never lit and nobody ever seemed to be in, and the house didn't feel a bit like a home.

It wasn't a bit like that in the winter. He liked it then. In the winter, his Mam always kept the place shining and spotless. The fire grate and oven and hobs would be black-leaded and so shiny you could almost see your face in them. And the hearth would always be as white as snow after she had scrubbed it and finished off with the chalk-stone, and there was always a big, red, roaring fire that you never ever wanted to move away from. The house even smelled cleaner in the winter. Yes, he thought, he'd definitely rather have winter than summer anytime. And the more he thought about it, he realised that all the good things that ever happened; the things you always looked forward to, all happened in the winter. Halloween, with Duck-Apple and roasted chestnuts, Bonfire Night, Christmas, they were all in the winter, weren't they? Yeah, there was the proof, he thought. Summer wasn't a patch on winter!

Another thing he'd noticed about summer nights was that they always seemed to make his Dad fight more with his Mam - much more than the dark nights did. Although, he reasoned, maybe it was too cold in the winter for fighting. But all the fights he'd ever seen between grown-up people had been in the light summer nights. The Orange Lodge for a start. There was always murder every July the Twelfth, between them and the Catholics, when they'd be marching up London Road past the Bullring tenements, banging their drums and playing *The Sons of the Sea* and *The Sash My Father Wore* on their flutes and concertinas.

And what about that time when he was still in the Infants, when gangs of men were going around smashing up all the Jews' shops - something to do with British soldiers being hanged in

Palestine or something? That was in the summer nights as well. Also, he recalled, that night a few years ago on the corner of their street, when he'd seen those big, hefty, tough-looking men in their singlets and their arms covered in tattoos, who had some other men pushed up against the wall, butting and punching hell out of them. There was blood everywhere, thick dark blood like he'd never seen before. And one man's face smashed in so horribly, and plastered with so much blood, that it had made him feel really sick. He'd never forget that night, because the next day he'd heard his Dad saying that they were the Peanut Gang from the South End, and that they were the most famous gang in the whole city, and that they never let anyone get away with anything. But, he reasoned, if it hadn't still been light at nine o'clock in the night, then he wouldn't have been playing out in the street so late. And if he hadn't been playing out, he wouldn't have seen that bloody fighting, which was so horrible and sickening. And who was to blame once again? Summer!

Even when Bernstein's furniture makers at the top end of their street went on fire, it was always during the light summer nights. But maybe that really didn't count because that place went on fire so often, that everyone said Bernstein used to set fire to it himself so he could get the insurance money. Nevertheless, he thought, it was still during the summer nights that it always happened.

Suddenly proud of himself for discovering the one thing all this misery, trouble and fighting had in common, he felt like some detective, who has effortlessly put all the pieces of a jigsaw together. He'd tell his Dad about that when he came in. He would be real proud of him for spotting the connection. On second thoughts, no he wouldn't. If anything, he wanted his

Dad's mind *off* trouble and fighting. And he didn't want to get the blame if trouble did start.

On the rickety table in the alcove next to the chimney breast, was an old Marconiphone wireless his Mam had bought at the auction rooms years ago, with some of the compensation money from one of her "accidents". It had needed a new battery for weeks, but she said they couldn't afford one. But this didn't stop Thomas from regularly getting the accumulator charged, so he could listen every Saturday to the football results - even though the power faded after about five minutes because of the weak battery.

Sheridan loved it when they had a new battery and a fully charged accumulator. The sound would be really powerful and he could listen to a new radio station he'd discovered called Radio Luxembourg. Unlike the BBC's Light Programme or, even worse, the Home Service, which only had old-fashioned programmes like *Grand Hotel*, *The Archers* and *Mrs Dale's Diary*, Radio Luxembourg played all the latest records from America.

Still waiting apprehensively for his Mam and Dad, he tried to break the tension by fiddling with the wireless dial, until he finally managed to get Luxembourg. But although the battery started fading again, he could hear very faintly Nat King Cole singing *Mona Lisa*. It was a song he liked so much that he wanted to learn the words. But as he started to pick them up with his ear close to the speaker, the sound became even fainter then faded out altogether. It was so frustrating.

He really wished they had electricity so they could listen to the wireless as much as they liked, whenever they liked. Or even an old wind-up gramophone would do, like the *His Master's Voice* one they used to have. But his Dad had taken that to the pawn shop one day and had then sold the pawn ticket, so that they could never get it back no matter how much money they had. But they still had the old secondhand records from that time, which he guessed must have become too scratched and worthless, otherwise his Dad would have pawned them too.

When they had the old gramophone, Sheridan used to play the records. But he found it so annoying to keep putting little needles in the arm for nearly every record, and to keep winding it up with a handle at the side. It was really old-fashioned. But at least, he thought, there was always a bit of music in the house. And you didn't have to keep buying batteries and getting accumulators charged all the time.

Most of the records were old-fashioned too, but there were several that he liked. The Strauss waltzes like the *Blue Danube* for one. And there was another by somebody called "The Street Singer" called, *The Masquerade Is Over*, which had on the other side a lovely song called *South Of The Border*. He'd liked those two so much he had even learned all the words.

It was so frustrating and so unfair to him that they still had all these records, but nothing to play them on. He really loved all kinds of music and really missed it. The house seemed so dead without music. He often thought that when he grew up and got married, he'd have, not just a wind-up gramophone, but big electric radiograms and pianos and guitars and all the latest records, and there would be music all day and night throughout the whole house. Where the money would come from to provide all this never bothered him, he was so certain that by that time he would be a famous singer - and singers were always loaded with money. And although he told himself that the shyness, which always made him feel so wretched and awkward, would have long disappeared by the time he was grown-up, he couldn't be absolutely certain. It nagged him deep down, this shyness. It seemed to be an obstacle, which would always stop him from getting what he wanted and spoil any true happiness.

On the very rare occasion, his Mam would take him to the *Pavilion* theatre, and as he sat enthralled by singers like Issy Bonn and Joseph Locke and Ronnie Ronalde, he would crave to get up there on the stage and give the audience one of his own songs. He was certain that if he'd done so, everyone would have been so surprised that they would have applauded him forever. Yet, he always sort of knew he was only kidding himself. He'd never have the nerve in a million years to get up on stage and sing in front of all those people. What if somebody from their street recognised him? He'd never be able to live it down. But, he insisted to himself, if the "Pivvy" was somewhere else really far away, like say, America, where nobody knew him, he wouldn't have thought twice about it. He knew he was good, and he wasn't really scared, but around here he just wouldn't have been able to face people afterwards.

One night his Mam took him to the Pivvy to see a man named Carroll Levis, who had a show called *Opportunity Knocks*. He guessed she had only taken him to see this show to get him interested in going on the stage, because whenever his Dad brought friends back from the pub for "jars out", she'd always tell them how good a singer he was and how he should be on the stage.

There were lots of kids on stage that night, and he thought he could have beaten any of them at singing... so long as it was in private. They were only up there, he thought, because they had no shame and were dead forward. To him they were no more than a bunch of show-offs. But then, out of the side of his eye, he'd caught his Mam looking at him with a kind of look, as if to say, "*You* should be up there." And it made him feel terrible, as if he'd really let her down.

After that, he didn't want to watch the rest of the show. It had made him so sad to see his Mam unhappy, he just wanted to get out of the place and forget all about going on the stage. That was when he realised that things would always be the same for them; he'd always be shy, and they'd always be poor, and things would never change. It would have felt so unreal if they ever did. But despite this wretched feeling, he kept a secret hope that one day his shyness would go. And when it did, and when he was really grown-up, he'd show them all. He'd be the best singer in the world, and the richest and the most famous. And by that time, he wouldn't be living in scruffy old Liverpool, where everybody knew him, so he'd have nothing to worry about.

Chapter Eight

His Mam and Dad mustn't have gone out till late, he thought, because there was a big pan of freshly made barley soup on the stove, that wasn't there when he'd left earlier. Deciding to get some down him before they came in, he lit the most powerful gas ring so it would warm up that much quicker.

One thing about his Mam, he thought warmly, she always cooked some scoff before she went out. And even though she never ate much herself, she always thought of other people. There was always something in the pan on the stove. It was like a permanent stock pot - even if it was usually cold.

At school he'd often argue with his mates about mams. Most of them had young mams. His Mam wasn't young, but he reckoned that the likes of her looked after you better than the younger mams. They didn't know how to make pans of soup and Scouse, and make things like roast dinners and apple tarts and scones and rhubarb pie. All they could do was give their kids cornflakes and send them to the Chippy for chips and fishcake for their tea, or else buy them loads of cream cakes. He thought maybe this was one of the reasons he, like his brothers, was the Cock - because his Mam knew what kind of stuff to feed them on to make them healthy and strong. On winter mornings - when she could afford enough fresh milk - she would always make him hot porridge oats. And everyone knew how strong that made you. But all the cissies with young mams: all they ever got was cold cornflakes or something like that.

Just as he was sitting down to enjoy the soup, he heard the sound of drunken voices at the front door. His Dad was singing as usual, but he could hear his Mam arguing with him. Grimly, he thought, this is it! Suddenly he didn't feel hungry anymore.

Banging on the knocker, his Dad was shouting, "Aye, aye! open the door!" Panicking, he raced down the lobby and let them in. His Dad, staggering slightly, bent down, put his heavy arms around him and hugged him tightly.

"Here's my lad", he lovingly declared. "Here's my lovely Sherry." Sheridan felt both happy and annoyed: happy because his Dad was in a good mood, but annoyed through again being called that nickname.

Once in the kitchen, he noticed his Mam's bag was empty: there was no ale in it tonight. But his Dad had two quart bottles stuck tight in his coat pockets, so he helped him to pull them out. Then, sitting down in the armchair, he said generously, "Go on son. Help yerself if yer want."

He got the impression his Dad had had enough ale. But, not wanting to appear too forward, reluctantly ignored the invitation. His Mam, sitting in the other armchair with her coat still on, then said, "No, he won't help himself." She wasn't all that drunk, but she was drunk enough to stand up to his Dad. "You shouldn't be encouraging the child", she went on. "D'yer want him to end up like you - a fuckin' drunkard?"

"Ah eh, Kate", he replied good-naturedly, "don't be like that girl. Won't do him any harm."

His Dad didn't seem to want any trouble. But that was the trouble thought Sheridan, if it wasn't him, it was her who started it.

"Anyway", he went on, "It'll do him good... best laxative in the world, mild ale."

"Oh, fuck off", she said dismissively, "He's only a baby. He doesn't need fuckin' laxatives."

"Yeah, I know that Kate,", he said, still amiable, "but it's nice to keep yer system in order. Why d'yer think I never suffer with constipation or piles or anything? Only because of the ale."

Sheridan always felt embarrassed and disgusted when they'd start talking like this. That's what made him so ashamed of their house. Things like having all broken boarded-up windows in the kitchen and bedrooms; like having no electricity like everybody else had; like mice and slugs all over the house... and the bucket upstairs of a night when they were drunk. Nothing was sacred to them when they were drunk. They had no shame or anything. Sometimes they were so bad, he wondered if they were really crazy.

"Ah eh, Kate", said his Dad still trying to be friendly despite her drunken sneering, "don't be like that. Let's be happy, eh?"

Sensing that he must have been hurt by the insult, Sheridan admired him for ignoring it and staying friendly with her. But she must have been drunker than he'd guessed, because she seemed determined to carry on with her nastiness and risk provoking him.

Fishing some cups out of the dirty bowl, Sheridan quickly wiped them with the old singlet they used as a tea towel, and asked his Mam if she would like a cupful of ale. Before she could reply, his Dad said encouragingly, "Yeah, go on, give yer mother a bevvy." He then started singing, as a sort of tribute to her, *If You Were The Only Girl In The World*. But as Sheridan offered her the cup, she knocked it out of his hand and sneered, "I don't want any of his poxy ale."

At that moment he could have killed her himself. All she had to do was just say nothing. Or just go to bed. But no, she had to keep it up. Surely, he thought, she realised what it would lead to? He began silently pleading inside himself as hard as he could, "Please! Please! Please! Don't Mam!"

He could almost feel her deep hostility, as she sat sneering and grimacing at his Dad. Yet, despite her, he carried on singing, seemingly carefree and unaware. But Sheridan sensed that he too must have felt it. So he knew he had to do or say something urgently, before everything exploded. "Aw eh, Mam", he begged, "Why d'yer have to be like that? Me Dad's happy enough. Why don't you be happy as well? Why don't yer have a song with him?" On hearing this, his Dad stopped singing, his face breaking out into a broad smile. "There yer are, Kate", he said, rubbing his hands gleefully, "There's yer youngest telling yer." Then, in a gesture of reconciliation, he leaned forward, putting his arms around her, and said, "Come on Kate, give us a song girl. Come on, give us, *The Sunshine Of Your Smile.*

This was his Mam's favourite song. She said it always reminded her of her brother Albert, who was only seventeen, when he was killed on the very last day of the War. He always used to sing it, she said, before joining up by lying about his age.

But she was in no mood for singing now. If anything, the mention of the song seemed to have made her even more morose, because she suddenly screamed at his Dad, "Fuck off. I hate yer!"

Something inside Sheridan then collapsed. He knew that finally this was it! It was unstoppable now. With all hope gone of trying to save the situation, he began crying with despair. His desperate tears were genuine, but neither of them took any notice. If anything, his tears seemed to fan the flames because, through his watery eyes, he caught sight of a mad horrible look creeping over his Dad's face as he jumped out of the chair and stood menacingly astride his Mam. In a desperate attempt to stave off the inevitable, Sheridan tried to get in between them and, with the tears now streaming down his face, begged, "No, Dad! Please no! Please, Dad! Please don't hit her, Dad!" But his Mam just sat there as if she hadn't seen or heard him. Then in a strangely calm, yet quietly defiant voice full of contempt, she said, "You're not a man. You're only a jack-twat."

That was when his Dad lost all control. "Ah! Fuck yer!" he cried in a mad rage, as he began punching her all around the head and body. The sound of the punches on her soft face were sickening, as he screamed at his Dad to stop. But he wouldn't.

His Mam, blood now trickling down from her head, and out of her nose, began howling and wailing like some crazed animal. It was an horrific sound of pure terror. Feeling cold all over, and trembling with fear, Sheridan felt paralysed and for a few moments couldn't move. And the more his Mam screamed, the more his Dad pummelled her, making him even more terrified.

Struggling to overcome his shock and fear, he ran over and again tried to get in between them to protect his Mam from any more blows, but could hardly see through the streaming tears.

"Ah please, Dad!" he cried, "Please don't hit her anymore. She didn't mean it. She's had enough! Please, Dad! Please!" But his Dad, now uncontrollable, roared at him, "Get out of my fuckin' way! I don't wanna hurt *you*!"

His Mam was still howling at the top of her voice like a mad woman. But although she was trapped in the chair, she was kicking out wildly as he continued to rain punches on her with his heavy fists. She then somehow managed to grab him by the hair, clinging to it with all of her might.

"You bastard!" he roared with pain, "Let go! Let go, yer fuckin' bastard!"

He seemed to be half-threatening and half-pleading with her. But she wouldn't let go. So, in desperation, he then began to really beat her up, as she howled even louder and began screaming hysterically, "Murder! Police! Police! Help! Murder!"

Witnessing the horrific spectacle, something snapped inside of Sheridan, and he began screaming at his Dad, as he tried to drag him off.

"You dirty old bastard!" he shrieked. "Leave her alone! Leave her alone, you fuckin' bastard!"

Pushing him aside, his Dad was now biting his Mam's arm in an attempt to release her tight grip on his hair. But she still wouldn't let go as she screamed, and yelled, "Get the police! Get the police!"

At first, he wasn't sure what to do for the best: whether to stay and try and stop it or run for the police. But with his Mam's terrifying screams ringing in his ears, and the horrible sight of her bloodied face, he knew he would have to get help, before his Dad killed her.

Racing up the street, he was shaking all over, his legs feeling as if they would buckle under him any second. As he turned the corner and ran along the main street to the police station, he was praying desperately for the sight of a uniform, whilst trying to wipe the streaming tears from his eyes. It was crazy to even think of it at a time like this, he thought, but he was really worried in case the policeman saw him crying because only cissies cried.

Suddenly, he spotted in the Chemist's shop doorway ahead, what seemed like the silver glint of a policeman's helmet, so he put a spurt on to reach it. But, without warning, he went flying onto the pavement. The cursed boots had tripped him up yet again. This, on top of everything else, was altogether too much for him. He went completely berserk, ripping off the boots as he sat on the pavement, and yelling, "Fuck yer! Fuck yer!" In this rage, he then ripped off the old tantalising socks and kicked them into the gutter. He didn't care about anyone or anything now, as he raced barefoot towards the Chemist's shop. The only thought in his head was to get a policeman.

It was a copper after all, he thought gratefully, and was so grateful he hadn't been seeing things.

"Hey, sir", he panted, "can yer come to our house quick, me Dad's murdering me Mam. He's killing her."

The tall, slim officer, calmly stood looking at him for a few seconds without speaking.

"Please, sir!" he pleaded in desperation, "If yer don't hurry up, he'll kill her. He's battered her already!"

But there was still no response from the constable. He didn't seem to realise how urgent it was. When he did finally speak, he asked suspiciously, "What are yer doing running around with no shoes and socks on?"

"They were just ripped and everything", he quickly explained. "Kept tripping me up, just threw them away,"

Why, he thought, was this stupid copper so worried about his shoes and socks, when his Mam was being battered to death. He didn't seem a bit worried. It was so maddening.

"Please sir", he implored, "can't yer please come with me to our house? He's nearly killing me Mam. There's blood all over the place!"

"Are you sure about this? Are you telling the truth? Or have yer been out robbing somewhere?"

He was now almost screaming at the policeman in exasperation. "No, I'm telling the truth. I wouldn't tell lies about something like that!"

What a pure bastard this copper was, he thought madly. He probably never had to suffer like this when he was a kid.

Now completely losing his temper, he screamed hysterically at the policeman, "If yer don't hurry up, he'll fuckin' kill her!"

"Alright, calm down", he said, still without a trace of sympathy. "And watch yer language. Whereabout d'yer live?"

"Down there", he frantically cried, "Two streets away, number thirty-five!"

"Oh! Your name's Connolly then, is it?" he said sarcastically. "Frank up to his old tricks again, is he? Don't know why yer mother doesn't bloody-well get away from him, the fuckin' head case."

The policeman had now taken his truncheon out of his pocket and was walking so fast Sheridan had to trot alongside to keep up with him. Right now, he hated his Dad for beating up his Mam, but he still hoped the copper wasn't going to harm him. As bad as his Dad was, he'd sooner have him any day than a copper.

When they reached their street, Sheridan saw two other policemen standing on the corner. He felt relieved, because at least this meant his Mam and Dad weren't fighting in the street. And there couldn't be much noise coming from the house either. Everyone had now gone home from the pubs and everywhere was quiet, so surely if his Mam was still screaming, these coppers would be able to hear it. He knew it was a lot to hope for, but maybe they'd actually stopped fighting. But then, the most terrifying feeling he had ever had in his life suddenly hit him with terrible force - what if he'd killed his Mam? What if his poor Mam was dead?

Like the policeman from the Chemist's doorway, one of the others was a Cornet. The other, who had a bike and was wearing shiny black leggings, was a Sandwich.

He and his mates had given them these nicknames, because the tall helmets worn by the constables were like ice-cream cornets, and the ones with flat peaked caps were like ice-cream wafer sandwiches. Of the two, he'd always thought the Sandwiches looked the smartest. Their uniforms, unlike the Cornets', who seemed to look silly in their tall helmets, seemed neater with their black gloves, smart leggings and peaked caps and everything. But the bigger lads around the neighbourhood called the Sandwiches the Gestapo, and said they were real bastards when they got you in the police station.

The two policemen, like the first one, didn't seem to be in any hurry as they talked to each other, with the Sandwich leaning on his bike. It was right, thought Sheridan, what his Mam always said about never being able to find a policeman when you want one. But when you do, it doesn't rain, it pours.

The way they just casually stood talking was making his blood boil and just as he was about to scream at them to do something, he heard the first Cornet say to the others, "Oh, it's only Frankie Connolly, at it again."

"Oh yeah, the bloody hero wife-beater", said the Sandwich.

Sheridan didn't know what they meant, but they seemed to be sneering at his Dad, as if he were some kind of a joke.

He hated policemen. They never cared about anyone and always seemed hell bent on spoiling everyone's fun. But he nevertheless really envied them. They were never a bit nervous or frightened or unhappy or anything. It must have been great just to be grown-up, he thought, but imagine being a grown-up and a copper! You'd never be afraid of anything in the whole world.

On the Sandwich's bike, under the crossbar, was a triangular saddlebag. All the Sandwiches had these, which were black and shiny and looked like leather. He didn't know what they were for or what they contained, but he'd often thought they were there simply to match their shiny leggings. Sort of like the caps and blazers the college puddings from the Hebrew school nearby wore. What made them match was the school badges on both, and what made the coppers gloves and leggings and saddlebags match, was their black shiny leather.

After murmuring to each other for a few more seconds, the Sandwich removed his truncheon from under the bike's crossbar and said to the others, "Right, let's get down there and have a gander. See what the prick's up to this time." He seemed to be the boss out of the three to Sheridan, as he noticed the three silver stripes on his tunic. But he didn't care, the main thing was that they were moving at last. And at least they were going to do *something*. Not like that bastard last year, when his Dad was threatening to kill his Mam with the bread knife.

He'd ran for the police that night too, half a mile all the way to the police station, only to be told that nothing could be done until his Dad had actually stabbed her. He was really disgusted when the copper had told him to go back home, wait for his Dad to knife his Mam, then come back and tell him. Up till that night, he'd always thought the police were there to *stop* the fighting and trouble. But it seemed to him they would only help after the damage was done, when it was too late. What kind of a police force is that, he thought. He'd always really hated coppers after that. When all was said and done, he thought, they couldn't care less how many mams were battered to death or how many homes were wrecked.

Reaching the front door, Sheridan was glad that the policemen were at last going to do something, but instead they stood listening for a few seconds. The screaming had stopped, but they could hear his Mam, between her whimpering, cursing like mad, calling his Dad all the filthy names under the sun. From the echoing sound, Sheridan guessed she was probably standing either in the lobby or on the dark stairs or landing.

"Do you know if he's got a weapon?" asked the Sandwich in a hushed tone. His manner had now changed. He no longer seemed bored or sarcastic or amused. At last, he was taking things seriously. "I don't know", he almost whispered, "I don't think so. I hid all the knives earlier on."

The front door was closed, and he felt terribly guilty for not leaving the latch on when he'd ran out. His Mam could have been killed behind that locked door.

Suddenly one of the Cornets was on the top step, rapping heavily on the cast iron knocker and shouting, "Open up, police! Police! Open up!"

Hearing the deafening knocks, his Mam again began screaming, "Help! Police! Murder!"

The sound immediately brought back the sickly fear and panic in Sheridan's stomach, not knowing whether she was being attacked again. The Sandwich now joined the Cornet on the top step and banged on the door with his gloved fist, whilst tightly gripping his truncheon with the other. "Police! Open up!" he shouted, "or we'll break the door down!"

Suddenly they all heard the sound of the bolt being pulled and his Dad appeared. Sheridan realised he must have bolted the door so his Mam couldn't get out. She must have felt trapped like a rat in there, he thought.

"Am I glad to see you fellas", said his Dad innocently. "Come in, come in.", he added, trying to appear harmless.

Sheridan was shocked at his appearance: hair all over the place, clumps torn out, his face covered in bloody scratches, and his blood-soaked shirt half ripped off his back - although the blood, he reckoned, was almost certainly his Mam's. Given the state his Dad was in, his attempt to appear normal and dignified seemed pathetic and ridiculous. And he was even more disgusted at the way he was crawling to the policemen, because he'd never seen him scared before. He'd always thought there was nobody in the world his Dad was scared of, and to see him like this was sickening. It made him feel sorry for him and ashamed of him, at the same time.

Brushing aside his assumed friendliness, the three policemen hustled his Dad inside and almost pushed him in the darkness along the lobby. Once inside the kitchen, Sheridan saw how much it had been wrecked, and realised his Mam must have put up a ferocious fight. The few windows which hadn't already been broken and boarded up, had been smashed, covering the floor with broken glass. And the greasy bowl and the big soup pan were lying among the glass, their contents of dirty dishes and greasy soup scattered all over the wet slippery floor. The hearth was covered in dark ale from the smashed quart bottles lying there. That was bad enough, but when he turned to look at the big sideboard, it was a picture of total devastation. The big main mirror was smashed to smithereens and the others either shattered or badly cracked.

The scene of chaos and destruction was so dangerous with Sheridan in his bare feet, that the Sandwich told him to put some shoes on. He didn't have any of his own, so he quickly went upstairs and put on a pair of Thomas's, even though they were far too big for him.

Back in the kitchen, one of the Cornets, flicking a broken cup out of his way with his truncheon, said off-handedly, "Been having a fine old time here Frank, haven't yer?"

His Dad had always seemed big and hefty and sort of invincible to Sheridan, especially when he was drunk. But now, alongside these massive coppers, he looked real small and dead scared. And his face, compared to their ruddy, fresh, healthy, hard faces, looked all too wretched and familiar, despite the blood and scratches.

"Now look, boys", he said, shrugging his shoulders, his hands outstretched pleadingly, "Yiz know I never look for trouble with you fellas. Biggest team in the world you'se are, and yiz do a bleedin' good job, I always say that about the police."

Despite his bloody, bedraggled appearance, and the scene of violence and destruction that the coppers knew he was responsible for, he was still trying to appear calm and dignified and normal. But although Sheridan sensed he was frightened of the coppers, he was still trying to suck up to them, acting as if he was an old friend of theirs, and that really sickened and disgusted him.

"Never mind the bullshit, Frank", said the Cornet. "Where's your missus?"

Anxious to get in first with his story, he said, "The woman's crazy. She's always like this when she's had a few bevvies, accusing me of other women all the time. God blimey, I lead a bleedin' dog's life with *her*." Just then, his Mam's voice began shouting from somewhere. "Go away yer fuckin' liar! Why don't yiz lock him up, the bastard. He can only hit a woman, the shithouse." Opening the kitchen door, the Sandwich shouted into the dark, "Okay missus, that'll be enough of the language. If yer don't keep quiet, we'll be locking *you* up."

It was all too much for Sheridan. These three big, strong, coppers filling up their kitchen with their authority and size; these strangers, who didn't seem to care a damn, standing there among the wreckage of their home, and his Mam still carrying on the terror; still acting like a wild animal. He couldn't hold back the tears any longer as, they silently streamed down his face once again.

"Look at the state she's got that lad in", said his Dad. "The poor kid's a nervous wreck."

Wherever his Mam was, she could hear every word spoken in the kitchen. Once more her shrill hysterical voice rang out. "Take no fuckin' notice of him, the sly bastard. It's him who's got him like that! He's got them terrified with his bullying, the drunken cunt!"

His Mam and Dad still seemed unconcerned about Sheridan and the effect all this was having on him. They were now more concerned about who was to blame for the trouble.

The Sandwich suddenly lost his temper and wrenched open the kitchen door. "Now look, missus", he shouted into the darkness, "that'll be just about enough from you! Anyway, get down here, so we can see yer!"

"No", she cried. "I'm frightened. He's got me and the lads terrified, he has."

"Never mind about that", he shouted, "Let's have yer down here. He's not going to touch yer now."

As the Sandwich continued coaxing his Mam into the kitchen, his Dad was urgently trying to explain his side of the story to the two Cornets. "This is the way it is all the time", he complained with an innocent, hopeless expression. Then, in an attempt to win them over, he quietly added, "Of course, her father died in the Asylum. Did yiz know that? In there for years he was. I think she must take after him, because she suffered with terrible pains in her head when she was a kid."

Hearing this, Sheridan was even more disgusted with his Dad. He didn't know if it was true, but even if it was, he didn't have to belittle and insult his own family to coppers. He was supposed to hate coppers, yet here he was trying to get pally with them by calling his Mam and his grandad all kinds of names. And if that wasn't bad enough, his Dad then dragged him into it.

"That lad there'll tell yer what she's like, won't yer Sherry lad?" Go on tell them. Isn't she always like this when she's got the ale down her?"

He didn't know what to say and silently cursed his Dad for putting him in this position. If he agreed he'd feel terrible about going against his Mam, because he really loved her. As far as he was concerned, she was the best in the world. And he knew she only got that way through drinking more than she could take, so that she wouldn't be scared of him. But if he contradicted his Dad and said no, he might be the cause of him getting put in gaol by the coppers, and that would be terrible too. And even if he didn't get taken away, he might hit him when the coppers left. Suddenly he felt responsible for everything that was going to happen now, and he hated everyone for putting such a heavy burden on him.

"You tell them lad", his Dad persisted. "Tell them who's the cause of all the trouble all the time." But before he could answer, the kitchen door suddenly flew wide open with a bang and his Mam appeared, waving her arms about and cursing like mad. She lunged at his Dad, but the Sandwich quickly grabbed her from behind around the waist and shouted at her to shut up or she would be arrested.

Sheridan could hardly recognise her. She looked grotesque. His heart went out to her, because he knew it wasn't her fault for looking like that. The flesh around her eyes was swollen and bruised, so purple it was almost black, and the skin was taut and shiny with soreness. And her eyes seemed to have almost disappeared, with only two slits in the swelling where her eyes should have been. And her nose, covered in dried blood, looked as if it was broken. It was flattened and seemed to be all over on one side of her face, and she had always had a beautiful, straight, delicate nose. Her lips were swollen and purple too, and at the corners of her mouth there were dried up flakes of blood. But the blood on her head was still wet. All her hair was matted with it. And her old pale blue pinafore, that she always wore, was saturated with patches of dark red blood.

She looked so helpless and pitiful, that he felt sick and heartbroken. Suddenly he felt within himself a deep rumbling of compassion and love. He wanted to protect her, rush into her arms and hug and cling to her for ever and ever. And it then occurred to him that, although you should have really enjoyed a feeling like that, he didn't. There was something about this atmosphere of horror and violence and sheer brutality that seemed to make such warm feelings wrong and out of place. Looking helplessly at this beaten-up pathetic figure, he couldn't believe that one human being could do so much damage to another human's person, even without resorting to weapons.

Perhaps, he thought, that's what makes it so evil. You could always blame the weapons and say people were not normally like that; that it was the weapon's fault. But when you actually saw what could be done between two human beings, without any horrible weapons; when you saw it for real, at first hand, done to someone you loved, it became sickening and terrifying and poxy and dirty. It was... what was the word his Dad always used about the prostitutes? Obscene. Yes, that's what it was, fuckin' well obscene. And it had turned his Dad into an animal. It must have done, because his Dad, who sang lovely songs to him; who gave him money for the pictures; who mended his boots for him; who kissed him with his stubbly chin when he was drunk and called him "my lovely son"; who was always saying how much he loved him; he couldn't have done this. He just couldn't have done! But deep down, he knew the horrible truth: his Dad did do it. And it made him shudder.

Suddenly, through his streaming tears he shouted, "He done that! He did! He punched her and punched her! And he kept punching her and kneeing her and kicking her, all round her head and her body and her shoulders and everywhere. He's always battering me Mam!"

He felt a tickling sensation inside his ears and gulped, as if he were choking. Then, he began trembling, and shaking his head in mad despair as more tears spilled down his face.

Everybody in the kitchen was now silent. They must have thought he'd gone mad, but he just couldn't stop himself. It was like when Thomas kept picking on him and hitting him, or like Freckles in the playground spitting in his face until he felt something snap inside his head. Then he wouldn't give a damn. He wouldn't care about anyone or anything, he'd just lose control and go mad.

His Mam began quietly sobbing, and he hoped that this time it was for him. And he heard his Dad calling him, "a dirty, lying, little bastard." Then he heard one of the policemen saying, "I think you'll have to come with us, Frank." But all the sounds seemed thousands of miles away. Nothing seemed real anymore. It was worse than a nightmare, because you could always wake up from a nightmare.

Chapter Nine

His Dad had been taken away about ten minutes ago by the Sandwich and one of the Cornets, but the other Cornet was still here, sitting in his Dad's armchair waiting for the ambulance to come for his Mam.

Sheridan was still shaking uncontrollably, too upset to worry about anything or even think straight. He'd gone past being ashamed of his Mam and Dad or the fighting or the state of the kitchen, but the Cornet said it would help a lot if he cleaned up the mess and made a cup of tea.

He didn't want the copper to know he was scared of the dark cellar, he wanted him and his Mam to see that, now his Dad wasn't here, he was fit enough to be the temporary Man of the House. The only problem, he thought, was that the Man of the House wouldn't be scared of a dark cellar or slugs or mice, so he braced himself to go down for a kettle of water. But, unaware of his fear, the Cornet then told him to get a bowl of clean water as well, to clean the blood off his mother's head and face.

Somehow he managed to get the water and put the kettle on. But although the uncontrollable shaking had stopped, he still felt weighed down with anxiety and misery, as he nervously watched the Cornet wiping the blood of his Mam's face with the cold wet flannel.

Suddenly, the seriousness of his Dad being pinched hit him. It was so unreal and bad enough as it was, but the thought of being responsible for his Dad being arrested made him frightened and deeply ashamed of himself. His Dad always said you should stick by your family. But after what he had shouted out to the coppers about him, he felt like a traitor and just wanted to lie down and die.

The happiness of the Hopey a few hours ago now seemed far away in the distant past. It was always like that, he thought hopelessly. Whenever you'd enjoyed yourself, or been really happy, something always happened to spoil it and knock all the goodness out of it, so that you felt you'd had no right to be happy in the first place.

His Mam was still whimpering and telling the copper she was all right. But he told her she looked a right mess and carried on bathing her face and head. She didn't seem to like a strange man touching her like this, especially a copper. She seemed to feel kind of uneasy like he did, and kept sort of brushing his hand away. He was suspicious when official people like coppers were kind and done things for you, because his Dad always said they were usually after something.

"If I were you, Mrs Connolly", said the Cornet, "I'd get him put away this time. If he gets away with it, he'll only do it again. It's not bloody fair, beating you up all the time like this." But she just carried on sniffling through her tears without answering.

Sheridan guessed the Cornet didn't really care what happened to his Mam, but was just trying to get around her so she would have his Dad sent to gaol. That's all coppers were fit for: putting people in gaol. He wished he had the guts to tell the Cornet to mind his own business and stop trying to turn his Mam against his Dad. But, even if he had the guts, who would take any notice of him? Nobody. He was sure of that, because whenever he opened his mouth - even when everything was quiet and friendly in the house and his Mam and Dad were just talking - he would be told not to interrupt, and that, "children should be seen and not heard."

Discovering all the teacups smashed, he wondered what to do. He didn't want to offer the policeman tea in an empty jam jar or Conny-onny tin. That was all right among themselves when they had no cups, but the copper wouldn't be used to drinking tea out of jam jars or Conny-onny tins. He'd probably think, "What a scruffy gang of bastards in that house." And he was fed up with people always looking down on their house and their family.

Still pondering how to serve the tea, he suddenly heard *Bless 'Em All* being whistled at the front door and it immediately lifted his spirits. He knew Thomas wouldn't have been able to fight his Dad or anything like that, but it still felt great to have your big brother, one of your own, here at last. It made him feel much more secure. At last, here was a face he knew, someone he could relate to, someone friendly and almost a grown-up, someone from his own family, and someone who would, at least, be sober. He never thought he'd see the time when he would be overjoyed to see Thomas coming through the door, but he was now.

In the kitchen Thomas looked shocked when he saw his Mam and gasped, "What's happened to her?!"

Quickly straightening up as if Thomas was going to be a challenge, the Cornet, towering above him, said "Now don't

get aerated. Calm down, there's nothing to get excited about."
Like the rest of the family, Thomas hated policemen, but he
took a particular a dislike to this one because of his manner.

"Who's getting aerated?" he snapped back. "I just wanna
know what's happened to me Mam, that's all." He seemed really
upset at the copper, who was acting as if he owned the house.

"Yer father attacked her", he said without feeling. "He's been
arrested and taken to the station." Then, pointing to the other
armchair, he said, "Go on now, sit down. Everything's under
control. We're just waiting for the ambulance." Ignoring him,
Thomas asked with a concerned expression, "Are yer alright,
Mam?" But the policeman answered for her. "Yeah, she'll be
all right", then added, "Which one are you?" More concerned
about his Mam than the copper's question, he absently replied,
"I'm Thomas."

Sheridan didn't see what it had to do with the Cornet who
Thomas was. The way they said it: "which one are you?" As
if you were just animals in a pack or something. That was the
trouble with coppers, he thought, no matter how much anyone
was hurt or how much chaos and panic and murder there
was, they couldn't take their minds off snooping and asking
questions. His Dad used to say that, when they joined the
police force, they were all injected with snake venom to turn
them into sly, cruel bastards.

This copper was really annoying to Thomas. He's just
trying to prove how big and important he is by treating me like
a little fuckin' kid, he thought. Well, I'm not a kid, and I'm not
fuckin' worried about him either. I'm a bleedin' man. I'll be in
the navy doing me National Service in a few months, fighting
for the likes of this cunt. So who the fuck is he to look down on
me? Then taking out his anger on Sheridan, he shouted, "Was
you in when it happened?"

"Now don't start picking on him", interrupted the Cornet. "He's been through enough for one night." Sheridan felt grateful, and relieved that at last there was somebody who understood how he felt. But he sensed the Cornet's attitude had certainly upset Thomas.

"I'm not picking on him. I'm entitled to speak to me brother, aren't I?" he retorted with a sullen look. He didn't seem a bit scared. The way he talked back to the Cornet surprised Sheridan. The Cornet seemed surprised too, because after that he never spoke another word until the ambulance arrived.

"You'd better come with us in case they keep her in", said the policeman to Thomas. Then nodding towards Sheridan, he said, "Will he be alright on his own here?"

"Yeah, he'll be alright, won't yer kid?"

"Yeah, I'll be alright", he agreed But in truth, after everything that had happened, he was frightened about being left in the house on his own.

When the ambulance men came in, the kitchen door and the front door were left wide open, so he could see the white ambulance outside with its blue light on top spinning around. He could also see several neighbours, who'd been aroused by the commotion, standing around the ambulance doors. What a right shower of nosey bastards, he thought. They all looked down on his family, he knew that. None of them ever knew what it was like to have fighting and trouble with the police or anything like that. But they loved it when someone else did. It gave them someone to look down on and something to gossip about.

The ambulance men were carrying a stretcher, but the policeman told them he didn't think it would be needed. He then went to help her out of the chair.

"Come on love", he said. "Let's get yer to the hospital and get yer seen to, eh?"

But, pulling at the policeman's sleeve, Thomas said, "Leave her. I'll take her out."

He seemed to resent the Cornet having hold of his Mam. And the Cornet took the hint as he stood to one side, leaving him to assist her along the lobby.

As he led her down the steps and into the ambulance, Thomas, on the verge of tears, shouted at the small group of curious onlookers, "Have yiz had enough now, yer gang of nosey bastards!" They all looked sheepish, but nobody said anything.

The Cornet and one of the ambulance men were the last to leave the house, and, as they walked along the lobby, Sheridan heard the short, stubby ambulance man say, "God blimey! What happened to her, had an argument with a bulldozer or something?" He seemed amused. Either that, he thought, or he liked to be familiar with coppers. "You'd think so, wouldn't yer?" said the Cornet. "No", he went on, "her husband's a right bastard... gave her a good thumping. We've got him though." He then added, "If yer ask me, I think the likes of her enjoys it half the bloody time."

"Seems that way, doesn't it?" said the ambulance man with a low snigger.

When the front door slammed behind them, Sheridan heard the ambulance pull away and went back into the kitchen. Everything was so quiet now, you could have heard a pin drop. The silence was so eerie. Exhausted, he sat on the edge of the tattered armchair still speckled with his Mam's blood, and sobbed his heart out.

⊰⊱⊰❍⊱⊰⊱

Chapter Ten

The following Monday morning Sheridan had to stay off school, because he had no shoes, but also because he had to look after the house, whilst his Mam went to the court over his Dad.

Any other day he wouldn't have minded staying off, but not today, because they always had Drama on Mondays, and he loved acting in plays. He thought Mr Henry must have reckoned he was good at it too, because he always gave him one of the main parts. He'd already been in *Treasure Island* and *David Copperfield* and *Oliver Twist*, even though those parts usually went to older or posher lads.

They didn't have a proper stage with curtains and costumes or make-up or anything, they just read the parts on the open, assembly hall stage from their drama books. The only thing that worried him was that everyone thought you were a cissy and a "mammy's lad" if you acted in plays, and because of this, he used to pretend he didn't really like acting and only did so because somebody had to do it. Nevertheless, he realised how odd it must have seemed to everyone that the Cock should be so fond of such a cissy's subject, because the Cock wasn't usually able to even read or write or do sums, never mind act. He guessed they must have thought he was a really strange Cock of the Class.

Before she left for the court, his Mam told him not to answer the front door to anybody because she was expecting the landlord to knock for his rent. "And", she added, "if you're a good lad and clean up and wash the dishes, I'll see if I can get yer a pair of shoes."

Her face was still badly bruised and her head was covered with a big bandage. But after putting on a bit of make-up and a head scarf, you'd hardly notice anything was wrong with her.

It was after three in the afternoon, closing time for the pubs, when she returned, and to his surprise, his Dad was with her. He was really pleased they'd let him out, but also felt scared about what he would do to him. But he needn't have worried because, although he looked half-drunk, his Dad was in a happy and friendly mood.

Seeming to sense Sheridan's fear, he hugged him tightly and said reassuringly with a tinge of grudging admiration, "Yer alright son, yer a good 'un. I've got nothing against yer, so don't be frightened of yer Dad. Yer looked after yer mother, and that's the right way... always look after yer mother."

Although they had both been drinking again this afternoon, they seemed to be genuinely happy and contented, and he hadn't seen them like that for ages. His Mam seemed to have forgiven his Dad, as she began emptying her shopping bags.

"What are yer having, Frank?" she asked. "Some fresh herrings, eh?"

"Yeah", he replied, sinking into the armchair with a contented expression, "that'll do fine, girl."

Sheridan was pleased to see all kinds of parcels coming out of her shopping bags, most of them in newspaper. They were food - sausages, liver, bacon bones and lamb necks she made soup with. But mostly fish: herrings, conger-eel, kippers and salt-fish. The whole room stank of fish. They were both mad about fish. She was never away from the fish market, and his Dad even had a saying about it: "Fish makes brains. Brains make money, to buy more fish."

Just when he thought she had taken everything out of the bags, she pulled out a brown paper parcel tied with string. He knew it must be something good because the fish and the sausages and liver and necks had all been just loosely wrapped in newspaper, but this looked *special,* as if it had been wrapped with great care.

Half-smiling at him with a sort of mischievous expression, she said, "Guess what I've got here for you?"

He was almost certain what it was, but pretended not to know, because she loved giving surprises and he didn't want to spoil it for her. So doing his best to look puzzled, he said, "I don't know. What is it?"

With her half-smile now broadening, his Mam unwrapped the parcel and slowly, teasingly pulled out, one after the other, a pair of brown shoes. "Try them on an see if they fit yer", she said with a satisfied look.

Eagerly grabbing them, he cried "Aw thanks, Mam!"

"Wait a minute", she said, pulling out yet another, but smaller, brown parcel. "here's a new pair of stockings to go with them."

This was altogether too much for him. His Dad back home and not sent to gaol; both of them dead happy and pally again;

loads of scoff for the week, and now brand new shoes and socks! All in one day! He felt like a millionaire!

The stockings were long grey ones with blue and red stripes across the tops, just like the posh kids always wore. Hastily putting them on, he revelled in their luxurious warmth and the smell of newness. But when he came to try on the shoes, his happy expression suddenly slumped when he saw they were secondhand. Seeing his disappointment, his Mam tried to console him. "They're not new Sheah, but they'll do yer a turn for a few weeks. The new ones were a terrible price."

He was sorry she had seen his disappointment. He must have seemed so ungrateful.

"They're a smashing shoe", said his Dad. "Wish I could've had a pair like that when I was a kid. Give them a good polishing and they'll be as good as new. Yer won't be able to tell the difference." Then, ignoring the scuffed toecaps, he added, "The uppers are perfect. And they don't need sole and heeling. Yer got a bargain there, Kate. Only been worn a few times, yer can see that. They're practically new."

He wanted to tell them both that he wasn't ungrateful, even if they were secondhand. It was just that he'd expected a new pair and he'd been more surprised than disappointed. But he didn't mind, they felt lovely and comfortable and warm, and he would really polish them up tonight for school in the morning. One thing for sure, he thought thankfully, he wouldn't be tripping up all the time from now on, and his feet would always be nice and warm and dry. He was so happy. Saturday night with all its terror and despair, now seemed just like a nightmare that had faded away and died. And with a huge feeling of warmth, he thought; really though, I've got the best Mam and Dad in the whole world.

"Now don't forget", she said, bringing him back to harsh reality, "no kicking cans in the street, otherwise they'll be off yer feet again in no time."

"Yeah", echoed his Dad, "start kicking tin cans around and they won't last a week."

He often played football with a tin can on the way home from school, and by the time he'd finished the can would be almost flattened out of all recognition. But although they were always telling him not do it, he couldn't see how simply kicking a can wore out your shoes as quickly as they said it did.

Rolling the cleaned-out herrings in flour on the kitchen table, his Mam asked if the landlord had been.

"I don't know whether it was him or the Gasman", he replied, "but someone was knocking just after you went out. Then, about one o'clock, someone was knocking again."

"Well", said his Dad emphatically, "the Gasman's paid for a start! We owe too much. Anyhow Kate", he added, "if they cut us off again, we've still got those two oil lamps in the cupboard. We'll have to make do with them till I get a few bob."

"It's not nice though, is it?" said his Mam. "I mean, I don't mind the light so much, we've put up with lamps before, but it's the cooking... know what I mean?"

"I know that girl, but it'll only be for a few weeks, and we've still got the oven and hob in the fire grate."

"And what about the rent, Frank? What about that?" she asked with a worried look.

His Dad was always complaining about landlords and how nobody should be allowed to own land, and something about "property being theft", so it wasn't surprising when he replied, "Oh, him? He can go and fuck himself. He's got no chance! When he fixes that leaking roof and puts proper doors and

windows in the rooms, he can start squealing about the rent."
His Dad seemed to have forgotten that it was he, who had
smashed most of the windows in the house, and had used the
bedroom doors for firewood. "Oh, it's alright you saying that",
she said, "but we might be put out on the street." But seeming
unwilling to lose his carefree mood, he casually said, "Fuck
him. Don't worry about it. There's worse things happened at
sea. The state of this place, he's lucky to get anything. It was
condemned years ago, we should be living rent-free. In fact, I
don't know about anything else, *he* should be paying *us* to live
here." Then, as if to reassure her and make her proud of him, he
added, "Don't worry girl, we've seen worse times than this and
we're still here, aren't we? Don't worry we'll get by." He then
suddenly began singing, which surprised Sheridan because he
hadn't seemed all that drunk. *I'll Get By As Long As I Have You.*
As he sang, he put his arms around her, hugging her tightly.
She seemed embarrassed and tried to push him away. Sheridan
didn't know whether it was because he was witnessing it, or
because she hadn't had as much ale as his Dad.

"Oh eh, Frank", she cried half-heartedly, "don't be soft. I'm
trying to cook the Tea." The flour off her hands was all over
his coat now. "Look", she said, "yer jacket's getting ruined."
But he took no notice and just carried on singing and hugging
her, and it seemed to Sheridan that, although she looked faintly
annoyed, she was really enjoying it. After all, it was better than
getting punched and kicked all around the room.

When his Dad next started singing an Al Jolson song, *When
You Were Sweet Sixteen*, it reminded Sheridan that he was on
the Hopey tonight. It would be great, he thought, if he could
go and be really sure of enjoying himself. His Mam and Dad
rarely argued or fought on a Monday night, because they were
usually sober. But even if they were drunk tonight, he reckoned

they'd really made it up with each other this time. Surely they weren't likely to start trouble again so soon after Saturday night? Yes, he felt sure he'd be able to enjoy *The Jolson Story* in peace and comfort, if only he could get his picture money from somewhere. Thinking of the various ways he might get it, he remembered there was still some wood in the cellar left over from Saturday. Already chopped up and bundled too. But it was much harder to sell firewood on Mondays, because they'd already supplied the posh houses on Saturday, and all the *working* people were usually dead skint of a Monday. The only reason his Mam had money was that she got her Assistance Board money today. At one time his Dad used to get it every Friday when he signed on the Dole, but he'd spent it on ale and said he'd lost it so many times, they didn't trust him anymore, so they gave it to his Mam instead, through the Post Office.

He thought about looking for some rags or jam jars to take to Slemen's rag shop around the corner, but then realised that the only two jam jars in the house were being used for cups, and that the last of the rags had gone last Wednesday for his Mam to buy the loaf and margarine and the fish paste and brawn for their Tea. Anyway, he thought, even if I had some rags and jam jars, I wouldn't take them to that bleedin' old miser Slemen: he only paid you a few coppers, even when you gave him loads of rags. Gentry's up in Paddington was much better. They paid lots more. Everyone went there. But, he thought, even if he'd had some rags, Gentry's was too far away to make it in time. They always closed at half-four, and it was nearly that now.

Finally, deciding that his only hope was his Mam, he realised he'd better be careful how he went about it, because once she refused you anything she'd never go back on her word. And it would be a disaster if she refused him, he'd never be able to see *The Jolson Story*: the Hopey was the last stop for films.

He'd discovered about his Mam that it was sometimes better just to throw a hint, instead of actually asking her for money outright. Because every time he asked, she'd just say, "Where d'yer think I'd get money from?" or something like that. He somehow sensed that she didn't like to think she was being taken advantage of. Either that or she didn't want to appear loaded in case Thomas started tapping her for cigarette money till payday. Or, even worse still, his Dad getting round her and pestering her until she finally went out on the ale with him and spent the lot. It must have been one of those reasons, he thought, because she wasn't mean, she'd give you her last penny if she thought you were stuck.

On the other hand, if he just sat there looking pitiful, she would always eventually ask him why he wasn't out playing with his mates, and that's when he would throw the hint. He'd tell her that *they* were going to the Rodney Youth Club or the swimming baths or the Funfair in Sefton Park or the Hopey, and that he couldn't go because he had no money. He wouldn't cry or whinge about it or anything, he'd just say it matter-of-factly. But inside he'd be on tenterhooks over whether she'd be touched enough to open her heart... and her purse. Usually, her good nature and sympathy for him would get the better of her. But he would still act unconcerned, as if he wasn't after anything. He'd found out that the more you pretend not to be worried about things, the more things you get.

Sometimes when he put on this act, or even tell her sob stories, he would still get nothing. That's when he knew she was genuinely skint. Today though, he sensed she must be loaded: buying a big load of scoff like that, and buying him shoes and new socks. A shilling would be chicken feed to her, she wouldn't even miss it. But he still didn't want to ask her and risk being refused.

He now decided to plant the idea in her head without further ado, because the sooner she was aware of his need, the more time she'd have to think about it, and, hopefully, become more and more sympathetic.

The herrings and potato scallops were now cooked and she told him and his Dad to sit over at the table. He wasn't keen on the herrings, because of the millions of bones that stopped you from properly enjoying them, so he just ate the fried scallops. She again said to his Dad, "Come on Frank, get yer Tea." So he pulled a chair over and sat down. Suddenly his Mam tapped her forehead remembering something, and said, "Oh! I forgot. We've got no bleedin' cups!"

Then, pulling her purse out of her pinafore pocket, she said, "Eh Sheah son, quick, run round to the Chandler's and get four cups."

As she handed him the ten-shilling note, his Dad said, "And don't forget to ask for chipped ones, d'yer hear?" Then added, "They don't half charge yer for perfect... the chipped ones are dead cheap."

"Yeah", said his Mam, glad of the suggestion. "Say, 'could I have four chipped teacups please' - what are yer gonna say?"

"Could I have four chipped teacups please", he repeated, as he went through the door.

"And don't forget the change!" she shouted after him. "That's a ten-bob note you've got there!"

"D'yer hear!" echoed his Dad, "That's a ten-bob note!"

He was glad they were pally again, but even that had its bad points: instead of one shouting at you and treating you like a baby, there was now two of them.

When he saw the ten-shilling note, he'd been tempted to ask if he could also get two penn'th worth of fades, but had stopped himself just in time. He'd have been a right mug to spoil his chances of getting his Hopey money for the sake of two pennies' worth of rotten apples.

Running to the Chandler's, the shoes and new socks felt great. At last, he could run properly without the fear of tripping up. He wasn't worried anymore about the shoes being secondhand. If anything, he thought, they were actually better than new ones, because new shoes were always tight and hurt your feet - but these didn't. And in any case, nobody but him would be able to tell the difference after he'd polished them. He was so happy and excited that, clenching his teeth so nobody would see his mouth moving, he began half-talking, half-singing to himself as he ran, "Hooray! Hooray! New shoes and socks, new shoes and socks, new shoes and socks..."

Taking his time in case he dropped the cups, he walked back instead of running. And when his Mam unwrapped the newspaper around them, she said, "Oh, they're handy enough aren't they, Frank?" Sheridan was glad she was pleased. And when he handed her the nine shillings change, she was even more pleased. "Oh, that's smashing that", she said. "Threepence each... couldn't get any cheaper than that." His Dad's fingers and mouth were smeared with grease and tiny bones, as he expertly picked at the herrings. "I don't know so much, Kate", he said, "those heavily chipped ones can cause disease yer know. Enamel's very hygienic, and if it's chipped off too much the germs get in on the pottery underneath. You'll always have to wash them in boiling water just to be on the safe side."

Looking at him with a mixture of surprise and annoyance, she said, "Well it was you who said get chipped ones!" She then brought the remainder of Sheridan's meal from the oven where it was being kept warm. "There yer are, son", she said, "finish yer Tea."

And despite him always leaving the fish, she added, "And watch them bones, pick them all out first, d'yer hear." His Dad said, considerately, "Come on girl, sit down an get yours." But she wanted to put Thomas's in the oven first. "He'll be starving when he comes in", she said, "didn't even have a cup of tea before he went out this morning. There was no milk."

"What are yer worrying about?" he said indignantly, "Won't do him any harm. God blimey, when we were kids, we were lucky to get a dry crust and a cup of cocoa of a morning... and no sugar *or* milk! And Breakfast! We never ever saw a bleedin' breakfast! Had to go begging for bread, we did." His Dad was always going on about how hard it had been when he was a kid. It seemed to Sheridan that it was almost becoming a like a sort of bragging, like he was somehow proud of it and that he was actually sorry things had changed. "I know all that, Frank", said his Mam, "but just because you had a rotten childhood... things were different them days."

Shrugging his shoulders in a harmless fashion, he said, "Does no one any harm, a bit of hunger. In fact, does yer good sometimes. Sharpens the wits, keeps yer system in good order, makes yer alert and appreciative and grateful. Yer know what they say, 'an empty belly an active mind'."

Sheridan could see his Mam slowly becoming irritated with his Dad - especially with him looking fit to burst, as he devoured the greasy herrings and scallops and thick slices of bread. No empty belly there! he thought. But his Mam didn't say anything more. She simply said in a mild tone, "Oh, we don't wanna hear about it. A child should enjoy it's childhood when it can." Then turning to face him, she went on, "Honest to God, Frank, I don't know how you can talk like that. I'd be ashamed to say I had to go begging for bread, while me mother was sitting in the house every day gluttoning herself with quarts of ale. She mustn't have been natural, your mother. An old drunkard, that's all she was." His Dad didn't get angry or lose his temper. He was well used to her calling his mother all kinds of names. But he had to admit she was speaking the truth: she *was* an old drunkard. But she was still his mother all the same. "She wasn't the only one, Kate", he said quietly. "There was thousands like her in Liverpool years ago. You know that yerself."

"Yeah, I know that, Frank", she replied. "We were always poverty-stricken as well, but me mam never let us go short of food. Even when me dad couldn't get a ship, she'd go out selling oranges or apples or *anything,* just to get something to eat for us, even if it was only a pan of blind scouse, or cabbage and bacon bones. She wasn't thinking about ale all the time. My mother would have died before she'd see us hungry."

Although they were sort of arguing, Sheridan wasn't frightened. It seemed a polite, even a friendly argument. He was almost positive there would be no fighting. And, as if to prove his hunch, his Dad suddenly heaved a big sigh and said, "Ah let's forget it shall we girl. Let's be happy, eh?"

Sheridan had waited long enough. Time was drawing on. It was time to make his move, to throw the hint. "Eh, Mam", he asked innocuously, "d'yer know where there's any rags?"

"What d'yer want rags for?" his Dad immediately responded. He was glad it was he who had asked because, although his Mam would hear his reply, it wouldn't dawn on her that she was the real target. "Oh, I'm just trying to get me Hopey money", he casually replied. "Why?" said his Dad, "How much is the Hopey?" Now this *was* a surprise! He'd never even thought about his Dad giving him the money. He was usually skint of a Monday. "Tenpence", he said, trying to sound as casual as possible. But, far from offering him any money, his Dad cried out in amazement, "Tenpence! Jesus! When I was a kid, we used to get in the *Rotunda* and the *Gaiety* for a penny. And twopence would get yer a big load of Jumbo toffee *and* yer entrance fee!"

He knew his Dad wasn't mean, that he'd just been making a comparison, but he still felt let down, because he'd thought for a moment he was going to give him the money. He also felt angry. The old bastard, he thought madly. Him and his fuckin' *Rotunda* and *Gaiety*, and his bare feet and dry crusts and cocoa. Why doesn't he keep his fuckin' mouth shut instead of spoiling everything. He's made it obvious now. He's ruined my plan. He's made it look at though I'm *asking* for my Hopey money. Well, I *am* asking for it. Of course, I am. I know that. But *she* didn't... not till he started going on about it. It was always the same, he thought, the ones who lectured you and questioned you upside down, were the ones who never gave you anything!

In the event, all the planning, all the anxiety, all the disappointment, anger and frustration were unnecessary. He need not have worried about a thing, because, without saying a word, his Mam pulled out her purse and gave him a shilling. All she said was, "I want yer back in the house before ten o'clock, d'yer hear me?"

After all the preparation, all the tension, he was stunned at how easy it had actually been. He'd never expected it to be *that* easy. Suddenly, it occurred to him that maybe she'd known all along what he was up to.

"And don't forget" she warned, "there's school in the morning. So don't forget, ten o'clock."

He was thrilled to bits. His Mam was great. Whenever she made you happy or gave you things or bought you anything, she always seemed dead casual and never made a big show about it. And the good feeling was made even better because of that.

Wanting to repay her kindness in some way, he asked, "D'yer want any messages, Mam?" It was a way of showing his thanks, the least he could do. But before she could reply his Dad said, "Yeah, yer can go and get me the *'Echo.'*"

He felt like saying, "I wasn't talking to you", but instead held out his hand, whilst his Dad fumbled in his trousers pocket for the money.

That was another thing he'd noticed too: the people who were good to you never asked for anything in return. It was always the ones who didn't care, who expected you to run around after them.

Since his Dad had nearly ruined his chance of getting his Hopey money, he decided it was now his turn to be awkward. Knowing the Final Edition wouldn't arrive in the shop until he'd left for the Hopey, he stated with a feeling of satisfaction, "The Final doesn't come up till ten to six."

But his Dad, who wasn't as drunk as he'd thought, said, "There's no Final today son. There's no racing today. Just get us the Late Edition" The crafty old bastard, he thought. That was the trouble with grown-up people, you could never really beat them, no matter what you did!

"Oh, give us the money then", he said, doing his best to hide his frustration.

When he arrived back with the *'Echo,* his Dad was talking to his Mam about some detective, calling him all kinds of names and telling her that this detective would have loved to have seen him getting six months. He quickly gathered they were talking about what had happened in court this morning.

"Did yer see his Jem Mace, when you refused to give evidence and walked out of the witness box?" he said with a smirk. "Sick as a fuckin' dog, he was." But before he could hear anymore, his Dad suddenly stopped and told him to go out and play.

"Yeah", she echoed, "go on out and play." It was the "children should be seen and not heard" thing all over again. It was always like that, he thought. Whenever they were talking about serious grown-up things, they always chased him out to play. He could never understand his Dad. During the day, or whenever he was sober, he'd call him old-fashioned and an "owld man" and chase him out to play. But of a night when he was drunk, no matter how late it was, he'd talk and talk to him and Thomas about all kinds of grown-up and important and dirty things. But he never seemed to think he was old-fashioned or an "owld man" then.

Leaving the house, he went and called for Reggie, but Reggie's mam shouted along the lobby, "He's not going out, he's having his Tea!"

"Can he come out after then?" he shouted back through the letter box, because the Palmers always kept *their* front door shut.

"No, he can't. He's staying in!"

He'd always had the impression that she didn't like him being mates with Reggie. "Fuck yer, yer fat old bastard", he whispered to himself as he jumped down the three steps.

He didn't know why they always kept their front door locked. It wasn't as if they were afraid of the Gasman or the landlord - he didn't think they were anyway. And it wasn't as if they were like his Mam and Dad - fighting all the time and scared of the police. They were very respectable, the Palmers, but, although she was Reggie's mam, he thought she was a miserable old cow. Didn't drink, never went anywhere, never even went out of the house - probably that's why she was so fat - and always dead nasty when you called for Reggie.

I'll bet it's because of me Mam and Dad on Saturday night, he thought. I'll bet that's why she won't let him come out with me. "You don't want to be knocking around with that scruffy Connolly", I'll bet that's what she's been telling him. "Get into trouble knocking around with the likes of that family." Anyway, Reggie was as bad, always taking notice of her. You'd think he was a little baby, with his mammy looking after him all the while, protecting him from bad people like me. I wouldn't mind, but he's just as bad as me. Worse if it come to that, with his swearing and the dirty stories he was always telling. Not only that, he even did real dirty things as well. Like last year when they were playing hide and seek, and he'd caught Valerie Wade down the back entry and took her knickers off and started feeling her and everything. What about that, he thought. That was something *he'd* never done. I'll bet his mam didn't know about that. Oh no, not her little baby Reggie. He wouldn't do dirty things like that would he? Of course, he wouldn't dream of snitching on Reggie. It just seemed wrong, the way his miserable fat mam always looked down on him and tried to keep Reggie away from him.

Freddy Owens was another of Sheridan's mates, so he decided to call for him. He lived in the end house at the very bottom of the street. But when his mam came to the door, she looked worried and said he wasn't home from school yet. He liked Mrs Owens. She was just the opposite to fat old Mrs Palmer. Thinner as well, more like his own Mam.

"He's probably stayed behind for Play Centre", he said. There was nothing in it for him, he just wanted to be helpful, because she looked so worried, and she was so nice.

"Oh aye, yeah", she said with a look of relief. "That's what he's most probably done."

She then asked, "Why didn't you go the Play Centre, Sheah?" he said, "I wish I could have", he replied, "but I haven't been to school today, and our teacher might've seen me."

"Oh, I see," she said half-smiling, then asked how his Mam was. "Haven't seen her for a while", she said. "Oh, she's alright", he replied. "She's in the house now, if yer want her."

But she simply shook her head, telling him it was all right.

He didn't know whether she'd heard the fighting and seen the police and the ambulance the other night. It didn't seem as if she had. She never said anything about it anyway. But even if she had, he didn't feel all that ashamed, because she herself was sometimes fighting with Freddy's dad. Only the other week, when he and Freddy were coming home from the swimming baths, he'd seen them both fighting like mad in the street. And Mr Owens, who was a huge man, was in his shirtsleeves effing and blinding outside the house at the top of his voice.

His Mam liked Mrs Owens. He'd often heard her talking about the time the Blitz was on, when he was a baby, when she would take him and Brendan and Thomas to the air raid shelter at the top of the street, and Mrs Owens would always be there with her kids. Mrs Owens and his Mam always stuck together and, whatever they had, they would share between them. He couldn't imagine that fat old Mrs Palmer ever being like that.

"Anyway, Sheridan", she said, going back inside, "I'll tell our Freddy yer called for him when he comes in."

"Yeah okay, thanks Mrs Owens."

He could tell by the size of her belly that Mr Owens had been doing it to her. Walking away, he felt a kind of thrill at knowing her secret. And she probably never even dreamed he knew. She wouldn't have stood at the front door talking to him so openly like that, if she'd known that he knew she'd got like that through Mr Owens lying on top of her in bed and sticking it in her. It always made him feel good in a funny kind of way, to know something that nobody ever thought you knew.

He hadn't believed Reggie when he'd told him about the things mams and dads did to each other in bed at night, and how babies were made and born and all that. And, he thought, he'd been right not to, because he had said that mams' bellies were cut open every time they had a baby and then sown up again afterwards. But he'd told him that was stupid. For a start, that would have meant Mrs McGovern having no belly left by now, because she had a gang of twelve kids! It was his Dad who had finally proved Reggie wrong, when he told him that night about the prostitutes and what *really happened.* But even then, he still couldn't imagine it. It really puzzled him and every time he thought about it, it made him feel slightly sick.

How dads could do that to mams, he'd never understand! Dads, he thought, must be real dirty bastards. And as if that wasn't bad enough, he'd seen grown-up men walking along the street with their wives whose bellies would be like barrage balloons. Everyone must have known what had gone on between them in bed, but they didn't seem a bit worried. They mustn't have had an ounce of shame. When he grew up and got married, he'd never be able to do something like that. He'd be too ashamed and shy. No sir, he thought, I'd never be able to that in a million years. Not ever!

Chapter Eleven

Sheridan was late for school the next morning, because the alarm clock didn't go off. And with the wireless not working, to know the *real* time, nobody was able to check how fast or slow it was.

On his way to school, at a street corner with the main road, was the bombed remains of what had been a large Georgian house. All that was left was the shell of the building and five stone steps, leading up to a massive square opening that used to be the front door. If you stood on the top step, you could see the clock tower of the University and its four-sided clock, which looked like Big Ben and was never wrong. So when he reached the bombed house and saw the clock he panicked: it was twenty past nine! He'd been late hundreds of times before, mostly through his Dad keeping him up talking way beyond bedtime, but he'd never been as late as this.

If you were only about five minutes late, you usually had time to sneak into the hall before Mr Wilkes, the Headmaster, began Assembly, because he and the teachers usually stayed in the staff room talking and drinking tea till then. But twenty past! he thought. He'd never be able to get away with it this morning.

The familiar feeling of dread assailed him as he broke first into a trot, then a full gallop. It wasn't the thought of the cane: the pain of the two strokes you always got soon went. And he had a knack anyway of letting his outstretched arm fall slightly downwards as the cane hit his hand, so that it didn't hurt as much as it was supposed to do. What worried him more, was the humiliation of being ordered onto the stage and getting caned in front of the whole school.

Now running like mad, he soon reached the deserted schoolyard and, after a brief pause to catch his breath, quickly climbed the six flights of stairs to the hall. Reaching the top, he thought, at least I won't be making a *full* exhibition of myself: at least my shoes and socks are okay, so no one can laugh at me. And that seemed to lessen the feeling of dread.

Peering through one of the small panes in the double doors, he could see the full Assembly facing him. They were singing *To Be A Pilgrim*. But because the "Lates" weren't allowed to enter the hall whilst a hymn was being sung, he had to stay outside. This made him feel totally isolated and excluded, and he cursed their clock for making him late.

The whole school singing hymns together was a lovely sound. And it made you feel so small and wretched, he thought, to have to creep inside on tip toe during the break and line up at the side of the open stage with the rest of the Lates. The teachers, standing around the walls, always stared at you as if you were some sort of monster and, holding a finger to their mouths, whispered "hush", even though you hadn't said a word. And all the other kids gave you smug, superior looks as if to say, "Look at that freak... he's a *Late*!" It made you feel you'd let the whole Assembly down and spoiled the goodness of everything.

When the hymn ended, he sheepishly crept inside and stood with the rest of the Lates. Mr Wilkes was saying, "Let us pray." But while most clasped their hands together and closed their eyes, some of the bigger lads, hidden from the teachers' view, started passing loose cigarettes and matches to each other.

When Assembly was nearing its end, the Lates were called one by one by Mr Wilkes onto the stage. He was holding a thick long cane, which had strips of black insulation tape along it with gaps in between.

There were nine Lates this morning, most of them regulars, like Sloppy Joe Flaherty. He was late almost every morning. And when it came to his turn, he shuffled up the two small wooden steps onto the stage, where the Headmaster was waiting, flexing the cane back and forth with both hands.

Flaherty, who had the nickname because he was always so sloppy and scruffy, was wearing an old pair of black plimsolls, which were torn and tied with bits of string instead of laces. And, because he was only wearing a jersey instead of a coat, everyone could see the large hole in the back of his pants as he faced Mr Wilkes. He seemed to be covered with holes, because his socks were also full of them. His face was clean but his neck was grey with dirt, and separating the two was a "tide mark" stretching from one ear to the other. All of this, together with his hair, which hadn't been combed, made him look like a real ragamuffin. And because everybody knew he was a bit backward, they all started tittering and giggling.

"Now that will be all, from all of you", commanded the Headmaster. And as the teachers peered searchingly along the lines, the giggling suddenly stopped.

Before each caning, Mr Wilkes always asked the reason for your lateness. But, as far as Flaherty was concerned, excuses were a waste of time. And as backward as he was, he seemed to know it, because, when asked, he simply stuttered, "Mmme mmmam ddidn't gget mme uup, ssir." Although he seemed to know excuses were hopeless, he still wore a pleading look. But Mr Wilkes just ignored him. "Right, come on", he ordered, flicking up his arm with the cane, so that it was outstretched with the palm facing upwards.

With his arm trembling in anticipation of what was to come, Flaherty looked like a little rag doll, as tall, slim Mr Wilkes towered over him. Then it suddenly came down with astonishing speed and terrible force. "Whhiisshh!" The crack of it could be heard all around the hall and silence descended over the entire Assembly.

He wasn't half laying it on this morning. He must be in a real bad temper. Everyone wondered why. One big lad from the top class whispered to his mate "Whoah! I'm staying out of *his* fuckin' way today!" And his mate whispered back, "Dirty long steak of paralysed piss! His fuckin' wife must have the rags up or summat."

Sheridan stood mesmerised as Sloppy Joe spun around and, squeezing the assaulted palm under his armpit, began hopping about with a shocked, agonised look on his face. He wasn't crying, but he was doing his best to hold back the tears.

"Come on, come on!" ordered Mr Wilkes impatiently, "Come on, the other one." Still shaking his palm and gasping with the pain, he held out the other arm as straight as he could.

It seemed to Sheridan that Mr Wilkes wanted to get it over with quickly and was getting angry, because he didn't want to be hated, and that he somehow knew that right now everybody in the hall hated him. But you had to admire Sloppy Joe, he thought, he might be backward and scruffy and all that, but he didn't half have some guts. By bravely holding out his other hand dead straight he seemed to be defying the Headmaster and everyone else in the hall - maybe because he sensed that none of them liked him. He seemed to be saying to everyone, "Fuck the lot of yiz!"

"Whhiisshh!" Flaherty's arm dropped slightly under the force of this blow and trembled for a few seconds. But this time he didn't jump about or anything, he just turned away with this hand now under the other armpit and shuffled towards the edge of the stage, his jaw muscles dancing with determination not to cry.

He'd taken the full force of the cane, thought Sheridan, without using any of the tricks himself and the others used to lessen the impact. He hadn't tried to dodge the cane or kid the caner. Okay, so maybe he was too thick to know how to. In that case, he deserved even more praise for taking it like he had. He was full of pity and admiration for Flaherty, and felt like rushing to him and telling him, "I don't care what these bastards think Joe, I'm gonna be your pal from now on so fuck them all." But just then, Flaherty tripped over and fell down the small flight of steps, landing flat on his face. The giggling Assembly now broke into outright laughter, as they watched him pick himself up and shuffle back through the lines, his eyes swimming with the tears that still didn't come out and his hands stinging like hell.

When it came to his turn, Sheridan hardly felt the pain. And what, he thought, was his own humiliation compared to Flaherty's? At least he was Cock of the Class, and he had shoes and socks on his feet, and was never out of the top three in class. But poor Sloppy Joe? What did he have?

Later, back in their class, Sheridan was feeling strangely rebellious, so deliberately started misbehaving - even in front of Mr Henry who had been so kind to him. Why should I be like the good fellas, he thought angrily. I'll always be looked down on as a wretch from a scruffy home, just like Flaherty. But what they can't figure out, is how I am just as clever as the teacher's pets and those well-dressed bastards from happy homes. Oh yeah, I saw the light in Wilksie's eyes when he was caning me - he really enjoyed it! But he doesn't know what to say when Mr Henry tells him how good I am at sums and spelling and poetry and geography. Oh no! he can't figure *that* out, can he? He still makes a fucking show of me in front of the whole fucking school! Well fuck him! And the school! And all the fuckin' teachers! If they want a real troublemaker, then that's what they're gonna get! Next time I get the cane and get made a public show of, it will be for *something*!

Mr Henry had ignored Sheridan's disruptive behaviour, because he didn't want to cause bad feelings and spoil the relationship between them, which seemed to have grown into a kind of respect - more on his part than Sheridan's. And if he could possibly help it, he didn't want to make the final move which would destroy it. But when he saw him for the second time blatantly throwing a pen across the classroom at Winston Sanders, he finally decided to act.

He knew he would feel he had betrayed the trust between them, but what else could he do? The boy was obviously only too aware of this special rapport between them and was exploiting it. But he couldn't let him get away with thinking he was someone special. Not only would that be disastrous for Sheridan, but also for the discipline of the whole class. He had to stop him right here and now. Either that or forfeit his authority and leave himself at the mercy of the rest of them.

Yet, despite his determination, he knew deep down that he was still treating Sheridan as special. For had it been anyone else, he would have walloped him with two of the best ages ago and sent him out of the class. But that was the trouble with this kid, and the thought nagged at him. He seemed to have a strange kind of dignity, which yet was threatening in a way you couldn't quite figure out. He seemed to know what was going on in your head. For a kid his age, it was uncanny. He knew the mere thought of it was crazy, yet the feeling was undeniable: he actually felt *afraid* of Sheridan. Not so much the mousy-haired spectre of a ten year old kid, but of what lay behind those dark, knowing, eyes. He sensed an abnormal maturity and sensitivity there. *That* was what was so frightening about this boy. And by invading that and showing his power, he felt he would be making for himself an enemy for life. But sadly, he determined discipline had to be maintained whatever the cost.

"Right, Connolly!" he shouted across the room, trying to look as strict as he sounded. "That's it! We've put up with quite enough! Down to Mr Wilkes's room and tell him you've been sent out of class."

Sheridan was stunned. Of all people, he never thought Mr Henry would turn against him like this. It was more embarrassing than anything else. "What for, sir?" he said with a mock expression of bewilderment.

"You know quite well what for." He was struggling to remain firm. "Go on", he added, "you heard what I said. The Headmaster's room. Now!"

Sheridan slowly rose from his desk and, to try and save face, made protesting noises as he left the classroom. He felt stupid at being chastised in front of the whole class like this. But what really hurt was Mr Henry turning against him so suddenly with such strictness.

So, he thought, he's just like the rest of them after all. And although he felt terribly let down, he also had a feeling of satisfaction. Well, at least I know exactly where I stand now... the two-faced bastard! "Your friends of today are your Judas tomorrow." That was one of his Dad's sayings, and he was dead right, he thought. All that palaver about poetry and everything, it was just a load of balls. He was only pumping me all along to find out more about me and my family, the nosey bastard. He's just the same as Wilksie and that poxy Miss Jones out of the Infants. But at least Wilksie and Jones weren't two-faced about it: they let you *know* they hated you. They didn't string you along, pretending to like you.

In one way, he was glad things had turned out like this, because he'd never be worried anymore about one day being caned by Mr Henry. Up till now the possibility of being caned by such a friendly teacher had filled him with a strange uncertainty. He'd often thought how embarrassing it would have been, not only for himself, but for Mr Henry too. But since he was now openly an enemy, it wouldn't have the slightest effect. It would be just like getting caned by Wilksie. And with Wilksie, you could always rob him of a lot of satisfaction by looking straight at him and letting him know you hated him for what he was doing. In a warlike mood, he thought, that fuckin' Henry can't have it both ways. If he wanted to be another Wilksie and act like an enemy, that's what he'll be from now on! I'll never ever trust him again. But losing something he knew would be lost forever somehow saddened him. It was like some part of his life had come to an end, and any kind of ending saddened him.

When Mr Wilkes asked you why you had been sent down, you couldn't deceive him. He would always find out later during the tea-drinking sessions in the staff room. So, when he asked, Sheridan blankly replied, "I threw a pen at Winston

Sanders, sir." Then, quickly looking around the study, he saw lying along the coat hooks on the wall, four long canes. The one he'd been hit with this morning was there, the one with the black insulation tape along it. Mr Wilkes had nicknamed it "Black Bess", and it seemed to hurt much more than the other canes. Two strokes of that hurt as much as six strokes of any of the others.

He felt certain that the Headmaster was going to use it. But, to his astonishment he didn't. Nor did he use any other cane. Instead, he seemed sympathetic, but, speaking in a matter-of-fact tone, tried not to show it.

"Now look here, Connolly", he said, "you're not a silly boy. You're always clean and tidy, and I know from your class reports you're quite intelligent..."

Oh, here we go again, he thought. Another lecture. I don't mind putting up with it, as long as I don't get caned. The trouble with him though, he gives you a long lecture and then still canes you!

"Now, you know and I know", he went on, "you're not like some of the more stupid ones. There's an excuse for them. Some are slow to learn and misbehave, because they don't know any better. Some misbehave just for the sake of it, But you? You're a clever lad, you know exactly what you're doing..."

Hurry up you old bastard! he thought. If you're gonna give me the cane, get it over with. He waited for Mr Wilkes to reach up to the coat hooks, but instead he continued with the lecture. "Now, if Mr Henry has to send you down here again, there'll be no second chances, you'll get four of the best with Bess." Then, as if to emphasise the seriousness of the situation, he raised his voice, "Do you understand, boy?" Nodding, he mumbled, "Yes, sir."

With his voice now lowered he said, "Now go on you daft bugger, get back to your class and act your bloody age!"

Sheridan happily raced back up the stairs three at a time. His estimation of Mr Wilkes had radically changed, the previous hostility and hatred replaced now by a tremendous feeling of warmth towards him. He hadn't seemed to even remember caning him this morning, yet he knew all about his good points. He realised he must have been wrong to hate him, and he felt really guilty for classing him as a cruel, hateful bastard. He even began to justify this morning's caning. I mean, he thought, I wasn't the only one to get caned was I? And *everyone* gets the cane for being late, not only me.

This changed thinking made him feel much better: as long as Mr Wilkes caning him wasn't a *personal* thing against him, as long as he regarded him as just another Late, then it wouldn't bother him how often he was caned. From now on, he wouldn't feel he was being singled out. Of course, he would still be ashamed of being caned in front of the school at Assembly. But he would no longer mind the actual caning, the pain of it, because he'd now know it wasn't because he was hated. So he determined there and then not to get the cane in future, if he could help it. The only trouble though, he thought, was you couldn't be a little goody-goody all the time when you were the Cock of the Class. The others expected you to be cheeky and to take chances, and you were bound to get the cane when you took chances and misbehaved. It was a lousy position to be in.

Although Sheridan had a new liking and respect for Mr Wilkes, his opinion of Mr Henry hadn't changed, he still hated him for turning against him so treacherously like that. And he had nothing to thank him for. After all, he thought, *he* didn't know Wilksie was going to let me off. Henry had turned against him, and he wouldn't forget *that* - especially since he had always been so friendly towards him. You expected that kind of thing from Wilksie or that Miss Jones, but not from someone like Henry.

Arriving back in the classroom with a confident smile on his face, he made his way to his desk, thinking that was the end of the matter. But he was sickened to discover it wasn't over. Sitting at his high Dickensian desk and still wearing a stern expression, Mr Henry asked him where he was going, and, before he could reply, ordered him to stand facing the blackboard with his back to the class.

It was so humiliating, and it felt so unfair. He never made anybody else do that after being sent to the Headmaster's room. And with Reggie and Freddy Owens and Winston Sanders watching, he felt so small and belittled.

He's only doing this, he thought, because he's twigged Wilksie let me off. He must be going mad because I didn't get the cane. It was like being hanged because all the firing squad had missed you! But he reckoned that no matter how guilty you were, if you were lucky enough to dodge one punishment, you should be let off! Mr Henry didn't seem to think that way though.

Spite! Fuckin' spite! That's all it is, he thought angrily. And in order to get his own back and try and reclaim some respect from his mates, he began making gestures and pulling faces at Mr Henry whenever his back was turned, and he soon had the whole class tittering. That really got on Mr Henry's nerves. But, he thought, there's not a thing he can do about it. For with him being the Cock of the Class, nobody would dare tell on him, and Henry couldn't very well cane the whole class *or* send them all down to Wilksie. I've got him fucked, he thought proudly, and the thought of it made him feel really great. Henry wanted a war, didn't he? Well, he's fuckin' well got one now!

When the bell rang for Playtime that afternoon, Mr Henry looked most relieved. His discomfort at having made an enemy of Sheridan was obvious. And he knew it. But Sheridan wondered if he would still be made to stand with his back to the class when they returned from Playtime. He had a hunch that Henry might now call off the war. He hoped so anyhow, it was no fun standing with your back to everyone all day like some dunce.

It so happened that Mr Henry was on playground duty and Sheridan suspected he would be watching him like a hawk for the least sign of bad behaviour, so that he could again send him to Mr Wilkes in the certain knowledge that this time he *would* be caned. So to deny him that satisfaction, he decided he would not take part in any games. Instead he, Reggie, Freddy and Winston Sanders merely stood by the school railings, rather than have their usual game of fun fighting. But as soon as the teacher moved down the schoolyard, Sheridan grabbed Winston Sanders by the collar and gave him a few slaps across the face.

"Aw what was that for, Sheah?" he moaned.

He was always like that, he thought. No guts or pride. And even when he complained about getting thumped, he always tried not to upset the thumper.

"Yer know what for", he replied. "Getting me sent down to Wilksie, that's what for."

"Aw eh Sheah, it wasn't my fault."

Sheridan knew it wasn't his fault, but after all the humiliations today, one after the other, he needed to remind them all he was still Cock of the Class.

The teachers always did the damage, he thought, making a holy show of you in front of your mates, then you had to go around giving some of them smacks across the gob to make them look up to you again. It occurred to him that you may win one day and the teachers may win the next day, but the other kids, they never win because they are what the contest is all about.

He valued his popularity among his mates more than anything, but he suspected it was only because he was the Cock: for them it was a good thing to be mates with the Cock. He knew his own value and he was determined to stay valuable. And that was the real reason he had belted Winston: to keep everyone else in line. He'd been feeling a little wary lately, and thought that if he didn't make an example of *somebody*, they'd all think he was becoming soft, especially with the teachers belittling him. In no time he'd be getting challenges from right and left. But, in truth, he hated having to play this role, because he hated fighting and having to live up to his title. But it was the only way to keep safe and secure in school and be free from bullying. If you couldn't fight, you led a dog's life.

Despite Winston's crawling attitude, in a curious way Sheridan liked him. He didn't know why, he just seemed to have a sort of glamorous air about him. Part of his attraction was that, when it came to music and all the latest records, Winston, who had electricity and a big radiogram in their house, was a real expert. And when Sheridan sometimes went home with him at lunchtimes, which he often did, they would always play Guy Mitchell or Frankie Laine records and talk about music.

He often thought how strange it was that he seemed to have something in common with each of his mates. With Winston it was music, with Reggie it was films and with Freddy it was plays. Even with the thickest kid in the class - Sloppy Joe Flaherty - he had something in common: their poorness and the holes in their shoes and socks. This feeling always filled him with confidence and pride - it couldn't only be *just* because he was Cock of the Class that they all liked him. But then, he couldn't really be sure. He remembered Freckles in the Infants, and the way all of his mates deserted *him* when he was no longer the Cock. Everyone battered Freckles these days. Even Flaherty could fight him.

Around this time there was a Frankie Laine record always being played on the wireless called, *Rose, Rose I Love You*. Winston had the record at home and had asked Sheridan if he also had it, because he'd been kidding Winston for months that he too had Lecky and a radiogram in their house. He felt he needed to tell these lies to the kids who didn't live near him, just like he pretended his Dad was a train driver. If he didn't make up these stories, he thought, he'd be looked down on as wretched and poor. And there wasn't one of them who was as poor as him, except perhaps Flaherty. They all had nice homes, even if they didn't all have Lecky. And all of their dads went to work.

"Yeah", he had lied to Winston, "we've had it for weeks."

"Smashing record, isn't it?" Winston had said.

"Yeah, it's okay", he'd muttered casually wanting to get off the subject because his neighbours Reggie and Freddy, who were standing nearby and who *did* have electricity and radios, knew that Sheridan didn't! And they might tell Winston when he wasn't around!

The prospect of Winston finding out that they only had gas and an old battery wireless that hardly ever worked worried him to death. I mean you could slap him around as much as you like, he thought, and he'd probably still bring you money and stuff if you threatened him. But you couldn't stop him from having Lecky and a radiogram and all the latest records. That was something you could never beat him at. When it came to nice homes and happiness, and good dads who had jobs, he knew he wasn't fit to lick Winston's boots. And the thought of it always filled him with wretchedness.

After being slapped, Winston pulled out a small paper bag containing some pear drops. "D'yer want one, Sheah?" he asked. With the others standing around, Sheridan snatched the bag out of his hand, and with a challenging look cheekily said, "Thanks. These are mine now aren't they?"

With a forced grin, and trying not to displease him, Winston pleaded, "Aw come on Sheah, yer don't have to take *all* of them. Yer can have half."

But, ignoring him, Sheridan began handing the pear drops out to everyone. And when Winston asked for one of his own sweets, he gave him a shove and said, "Go on, fuck off. Yer not playing with us anymore." Winston didn't argue. He didn't want any more slaps. Not only that, he even got fed up with his own grovelling sometimes. It was all right if nobody twigged you were a crawler. But once they found you out, nothing was any good anymore. It was just like now: having the power of loads of sweets one minute, then suddenly having none. So he took the hint and slunk away, melting into the crowded schoolyard, hoping to play with some other kids who didn't know how much of a coward he was.

Sheridan felt really powerful, and when Reggie and Freddy started laughing at the way he'd robbed Winston's sweets, he felt even better. At times like this, it was great being the Cock.

When the laughter died down, he began telling them all how great *The Jolson Story* had been last night on the Hopey. And he soon had them roaring with laughter once again, when he told them of how he'd just strolled into the Hopey after Old Alf, had shit himself when he'd threatened to tell the N.A.B. about him being paid for working there.

Reggie especially was pleased about this, realising that in future, so long as he was with him, he'd never again have to wait outside in the cold and rain begging people to take him in. But he'd have to be with Sheridan: on his own he'd never be able to threaten the doorman like that - it might get back to his dad. And his dad always told him that if he ever got into trouble with the police or anything like that, he'd take his buckled belt and strap his arse till it was red raw.

They were all laughing and Reggie was congratulating Sheridan for scaring off Old Alf, when Freddy, who never ever said much, suddenly spoilt their enjoyment. "But what if he gets the sack?" he quietly asked, "You won't be able to snitch on him anymore, will yer? There'll be a different doorman then."

Suddenly the laughter stopped. Sheridan hadn't thought of that. And before he could really think about the implications, he spotted three lads jumping on Flaherty's back and pulling his arms up behind his back and spitting in his face. Flaherty was simply standing there like a scarecrow, frightened as hell, as they dragged him this way and that.

What especially angered Sheridan was that the three tormentors were well-dressed kids, who never got into any trouble, and who were always "yes-sir-ing" and "no-sir-ing" the teachers. They were the same ones who were the first with their hands up whenever pens and exercise books needed to be given out or errands done or volunteers for anything. In front of the teachers, they were so well behaved.

Mr Henry was down the bottom end of the schoolyard, examining a big lad's fingers for nicotine stains after somebody had snitched on him for smoking in the toilets.

"Hey, Freddy", cried Sheridan "keep douse for old Henry will yer!" Then turning to Reggie, he said, "Come on, let's do them bastards." As they moved to Flaherty's rescue, his three tormentors tried to run away. But, grabbing them, the two friends threw them to the ground and began kicking them. Flaherty, his face and matted hair covered in spittle, stood motionless looking bewildered, as one of the three pleaded they were only playing in fun. But Sheridan ignored his pleas and forcefully kicked his behind. The kick caught the base of the lad's spine, causing him to roll over on the gravel surface, screaming in agony as the other two struggled to their feet and scurried away.

Seeing Mr Henry now coming up the yard, Sheridan halted his attack on the boy on the ground. But, clenching his fist at him, he quietly snarled, "Open yer fuckin' mouth and snitch on us, and we'll fuckin' kill yer at four o'clock." The boy, still howling like mad, didn't seem to hear. Or if he did, he didn't seem to take any notice, so Reggie bent down and whispered in his ear, "Listen cunt, you'd better say yer fell over or you've had it at four o'clock." The boy was terrified and still sobbing, but he managed to whimper, "Okay."

As they all casually disappeared into the crowded schoolyard, Flaherty stood transfixed, like a shocked scarecrow. He couldn't believe what had happened. Not about being picked on and attacked. He had got used to that sort of stuff: everybody always picked on him whenever they liked. But the Cock sticking up for him like that! Nobody had ever done anything like that before, never mind the Cock of the Class! Fancy that, eh?

For the first time in his life, Sloppy Joe Flaherty felt really important. It was a smashing feeling.

Chapter Twelve

1951

Not three hundred yards from Sheridan's home, at the junction of two main roads, was St Stephen's Methodist church. Twice a week, on Monday and Wednesday evenings, they held Cubs and Boy Scouts there in the cellars beneath the church, which had been used as air raid shelters during the war.

When he discovered that Reggie and Freddy had joined the Cubs, he was jealous and called them sly bastards for joining without telling him. Now he too wanted to join, because when their school broke up for the six weeks' summer holidays, there was going to be celebrations and fireworks and parades and parties all over the city. It was going to part of something called the Festival of Britain, and by the accounts he'd read in the paper, it was going to last for weeks and be really great. And if you were in the Cubs or the Scouts or the Sea Cadets or the Boys' Brigade, he thought, you'd probably be in some band or procession - especially if you were as fond of music as he was. And if you were, your Mam and Dad wouldn't half be proud of you. He could already see himself in his smart Cubs' uniform, marching along Lime Street past St George's Hall in front of the huge crowds of spectators, playing the bugle or maybe even as a drummer boy!

The problem was he wasn't allowed to join anything without telling his Dad. So as soon as four o'clock arrived, he rushed straight home from school to ask him.

It was Wednesday, the day his Dad was always in and sober. But it was also the day he was always narky and bad-tempered. Normally, he would have put off asking him for anything until he was drunk, but it was Cubs' Night tonight and he really wanted to be as good as Reggie and Freddy and join as quickly as he could.

In the kitchen he was met with the depressing sight of his Mam doing the weekly washing, which she always did on Wednesdays.

At one time she used to go to the Washhouse, but for some reason she'd stopped going. He thought it was probably because the load of wet washing she had to carry back on her head was too heavy. After all, the Washhouse was quite a distance away.

The big aluminum bucket with clothes boiling in it was standing on the cooker, while she scrubbed a pair of Thomas's dungarees on the bare kitchen table, which was covered in grey soapy suds.

Wednesdays always made him feel so miserable. Everything, he thought, seemed so bare, and all you could see was steam and all you could smell was soap and disinfectant and sweat, and there was never a sign of any scoff, and his Mam and Dad were always dead miserable.

With it being June and roasting hot outside, there was no fire lit. But his Dad was sitting in the old armchair by the fireplace, mooching through the old Diddy Box and looking really scruffy. He hadn't had a shave for days. And, although he was wearing a shirt, he'd taken out the front and back studs so that he had no collar, and this made him look stupid as well as scruffy. His hair was all over the place too, wild and woolly, making him look even more unkempt, as he searched intently among the old photos and documents.

Sheridan guessed he wasn't really looking for anything in particular but was simply passing the time away. He was always mooching in the box and through the dresser drawers when he had nothing to do.

"What's up with you?" said his Mam testily. "Yer home early, aren't yer? Yer Tea won't be ready for ages yet."

Might as well get it over with, he thought, looking warily at his Dad, who was still pre-occupied with the box.

"I wanna join the Cubs", he said loudly so he could hear.

Sweating with the effort of the scrubbing, his Mam said, "You'd better ask yer father."

"Ask his father what?" said his Dad, breaking his concentration.

Adopting a pitiful expression he said, "Reggie and Freddy Owens have joined the Cubs in St Stephens. It's Cubs' Night tonight, so I was wondering if I could go too?"

His voice was a whisper and his manner as humble as it could be, like it always was when he was after favours or money.

"The Cubs?!" his Dad roared with a horrible look of disgust, "The fuckin' Cubs?!"

The way he said was terrible.

"D'yer wanna get yer fuckin' ring snatched?!" he roared again. "Yer silly little cunt. Yer can fuckin' read, can't yer?

Don't yer ever read the papers?" He was really shocked at this outburst. He'd expected his Dad to be narky, with it being Wednesday and all that, but he hadn't expected him to be really angry like this, roaring and shouting like this. He was also puzzled and couldn't understand what he was talking about. He seemed to be talking in double-dutch.

His Mam stopped scrubbing and said reprovingly, "Now eh Frank, there's no need fer that. He's only asked a civil question. No need to roar and curse at him like that."

Becoming angrier now, his Dad leapt out of the armchair, the old box falling off his knee and spilling its contents all over the wet floor. At this Sheridan became even more frightened, thinking he would be blamed for the box falling on the floor.

"What the fuck's it got to do with you?" he roared at her "Yer want him to be turned into a fuckin' queer or something, do yer?" His Mam was trying to keep calm and not show her fear, telling him not to be silly and that the Cubs was harmless. This seemed to have some effect. He seemed to realise he was getting too worked up, so he sat down again. But the respite was short lived as he quietly, with a determined look, beckoned Sheridan.

"Come here, lad", he said with deceptive kindness.

"What, Dad?" he asked nervously.

"You read the newspapers, don't yer?" he said disarmingly.

Sensing what he was up to, and forgetting her fear, his Mam shouted, "Now you fuckin' well leave him alone yer dirty-minded bastard! No, he doesn't read the fuckin' poxy *News of the World*, and he's not going to. If that's what yer getting at!" Then, as an afterthought, she added, "Yer just wanna corrupt him, like yer corrupted the other two." Now becoming agitated again, he shouted back, "I'm fuckin' educating him! D'yer want him to be a little lamb led to the fuckin' slaughter?!" This new severe tone quietened her. Hoping she'd stay that way, he calmed down again and said, "You know fuck all about it, so keep yer mouth shut. He'd grow up to be a bleedin' puff if it was up to you, yer stupid fuckin' cow." Then turning to Sheridan, he gently asked, "Yer can read, can't yer lad? Don't yer ever read the likes of the *News of the World*?" Unconsciously, making a liar of his Mam, he nodded and mumbled, "Sometimes, yeah."

"Well haven't yer read about all those vicars and scoutmasters? They love playing around with little boys..." Now fearlessly interrupting, his Mam screamed, "Ah fuck yer! Yer fuckin' disgusting for a father!" But ignoring her, he finally lost his temper and roared, "They wanna stick their prick up yer arse, yer stupid little cunt!"

Sheridan heard them yelling at each other but was too shocked to make out anything further. It was just a cacophony of horrible frightening noise and a haze of red. His head was pounding as if it were going to burst, and strangely he suddenly seemed to have gone deaf.

Unaware of what he was doing now, he felt himself running along the lobby and up their street; running, running, not knowing where, his eyes awash with blinding tears.

He must have looked really weird, because a few times he saw worried faces and heard voices calling out, "Eh, what's up?" and, "Where are *you* going?" But he took no notice and just kept on running. He was in a blind fury of shock and anger, and his chest felt as if it was about to explode with rage and breathlessness, but still he kept on running.

When he finally came to his senses, he could see big posh cars cruising in and out of this bridge-like driveway in front of a huge white building, and women, really posh women, wearing fur coats, and men with smart dark shiny suits and stiff white shirts, going in and out of these big glass revolving doors. He then realised with amazement that he must have run for miles, because he was now downtown standing outside the luxurious *Adelphi Hotel* on Lime Street.

As he glanced across Lime Street to the *Palais-de Luxe*, his thoughts, for some reason, wandered wistfully to Brendan, and how safe it must feel to be grown-up. Then, the sight of the rich grown-ups, who didn't have a care in the world, going in and out of the *Adelphi* made his eyes fill with tears and, although he didn't shed them, he felt stupid and ashamed because people passing by were all staring at him.

"Hey sonny, wassa matter, huh?" Before he looked up, he knew it was the voice of an American. He'd heard lots of similar voices when there were loads of Yanks stationed in some of the of the big posh houses around Abercromby Square. All the kids used to ask them, "Any gum, chum?" and some of them would reply, "Not a stick, Dick." Mostly they were always kind and would say things like, "Sure, kid. Here's some candy." He remembered often being given "candy" and being surprised to find it was simply the American word for chocolate and sweets. Up till then he'd always thought candy was some special sort of American toffee.

The soldier was with a well-dressed woman, who had her arm in his. And as he ruffled Sheridan's hair, she tugged at his sleeve saying, "Come on, darling." She was very pretty and spoke in a nice kind of posh English voice. But for all that, he sensed she didn't want to be seen talking to a scruffy little kid like him. So, to spite her, he decided to talk to the soldier, so he wouldn't leave as she wanted. But, when he asked why he seemed so lost, he was too ashamed to tell him about the dirty, filthy things his Dad had said - especially with the woman standing there - so he lied that his big brother had hit him and chased him out of the house. And when he asked him where his parents where, he lied again, saying his Mam was in hospital and his Dad was dead. The soldier said, "Aw gee, poor kid", and began fumbling in his trouser pocket. The woman, who seemed to be getting restless, was now pulling at his sleeve again, but he didn't even turn his head. He just kept looking down at Sheridan and said to her with a smile, "Hold on a minute, baby." Then, finally drawing his hand from his pocket, he said, "There y'are, sonny, you go along and buy yourself some candy and ice-cream, huh." He then ran his fingers again through Sheridan's hair and grinned warmly, as the woman, becoming really annoyed now, pleaded, "Come on Stu. Please!"

When he looked at the piece of paper the American had thrust into his hand, Sheridan was so shocked he could hardly speak. He had given him a ten-shilling note! He'd never had that much money in his whole life. It seemed terrible that the only way you could thank people was with words. But he still cried out with surprise, "Aw thanks, mister! Aw thanks very much, mister!" The soldier smiled at him for several moments, before finally giving in to the woman's pleas. But as they left, he called over his shoulder, "And you tell that goddam brother of yours, Uncle Stewart said to keep his mitts to hisself. Okay?"

As the couple gradually faded away down busy Lime Street, he stood in a daze for what seemed like ages. And when he recovered from the shock, he felt so nervous and excited he couldn't keep still. He just had to move to somewhere... anywhere!

Walking up Brownlow Hill at the side of the *Adelphi*, he clutched the ten-shilling note in his pocket, his mind crammed deleriously with all of the things he could now afford, and all the things he could do, and all the places he could go. Without any effort, he realised that just one of the things he could do would be to go to McDonough's, where you didn't need sweet coupons, and buy twenty bars of Williamson's toffee. Just imagine that! he thought, twenty bars! And that was only *one* thing you could do. For instance, basking in this wonderful, relaxed, feeling of power and luxury, he thought, I could go in the One and Sixes in the Hopey and still buy five bars of Williamson's... and still have enough money to buy twelve iceys! The choices were gloriously endless. It was about the most smashing thing in the world to have so much money. There was only one other feeling as good, and that was deciding how you were going to spend it. In this delirious state it suddenly came to him that, if he wanted to, if he really wanted to spend the whole ten shillings in one go, he could buy one hundred and twenty lolly ices! This awesome thought nearly made him faint.

Even though Brownlow Hill was very steep, he began to hop and skip and run with sheer happiness, thinking what a smashing fella the soldier was, and thinking that, from now on, till the day he died, he'd always love American soldiers.

As it turned out, because he'd had no Tea, the first thing he treated himself to was fish and chips. Then, leaving the chip shop, he felt mean for only spending a shilling, so he went back inside and asked for a bottle of Cream Soda, even though he knew he would never drink it all. And after taking only a few swigs, he threw the bottle away as he passed a small bombed site, not even bothering to taking it back to get the threepence deposit. He soon got fed up with the fish and chips too, so he threw the soggy parcel of remains into the gutter.

He was more full up with excitement than food. It was the same kind of full up he'd felt when Mr Henry had given him all those poetry books. But throwing the fish and chips away, it occurred to him how you always enjoyed the little scarce bit much more than the large pile you got dead easy. Like when Thomas sometimes sent him on a Friday night for "four penn'th and a fish", he'd really enjoy the few chips he stole on his way back - even though Thomas would always smell his breath and give him a smack across the face.

There was a Funfair in Sefton Park and Mario Lanza was on the Hopey in *That Midnight Kiss*. The dilemma was: which one to go to? He was dying to see the Mario Lanza picture, and he might not get another chance to see it because it was only on for Monday Tuesday and Wednesday, and the Hopey only showed pictures that had already been shown everywhere else. It was a kind of last stop for a film. On the other hand, he thought, the Fair would be really great: he loved the Dodgems and Big Waltzer, and, though it sometimes made him dizzy and sick, it was worth it because on its loudspeakers they always played all the latest music.

Unable to make up his mind, he decided to toss a penny coin. Heads the Hopey, tails the Fair. It was heads. But the Hopey wouldn't even be open for another hour and a half. But if he went to the Fair, he knew he'd be going on every ride and would be skint after an hour and a half and then have to go home. And he hated having to go home early from anywhere when you were enjoying yourself - even more so after what had happened earlier on.

Anyway, he thought, I've made up my mind now. The only problem was how to kill the time till the Hopey opened, because he definitely wasn't going back to their house this early... if ever!

The sudden thought of their house and his dirty-minded Dad hit him in the belly, filling him with apprehension and nausea. And as he burped, he felt the sweet sickly taste of the Cream Soda in his throat combining with the greasy aftertaste of the fish and chips. And, although he tried to push the dread out of his mind, it lingered in the background nagging at him.

It was only when he was finally sitting in the Hopey that the sickly misery began to leave. For he was now lost in the wonderful, musical, Technicolor world of Mario Lanza, and the beautiful Kathryn Grayson, who he had immediately fallen in love with.

There weren't many in the Hopey tonight. The wooden pews of the Tenpennies were almost deserted. But, even though he could afford to, he wouldn't go in the comfortable One and Sixes where there were more people. He still preferred to stick to the Tenpennies. And this somehow made him feel proud of himself. It was the feeling of somehow being loyal that made him feel so good. But precisely who or what he was being loyal to, he didn't know.

When the Big Picture ended in the First House, he was about to leave, but on his way out, he recklessly decided to buy yet another sixpenny ice-cream off Old Lizzie. Then, letting his recklessness run riot, he suddenly decided to go back and watch the supporting programme all over again.

No wonder Lizzie always wore the socks on her hands, he thought. The tub of ice cream was freezing and as hard as rock. Nevertheless, he loved it when it was like that, because it not only tasted smashing as it melted on your tongue, but it lasted longer too.

Sitting through the *Gaumont British News*, he began feeling the edges of the coins in his pocket and thinking of how great it was going to be in school tomorrow. He'd be the richest kid in the school. And at Playtime, he'd get Reggie and Freddy to sneak out with him over to Darby's shop, and he'd treat them to penny drinks and toffee apples and Trebor chews, and they'd think he was really important. He'd even be able to show up Winston Sanders for a change, because the most he ever brought to school was sixpence... and what was a lousy tanner compared to his ten-bob?

The second showing of *That Midnight Kiss* was only half-way through but, although dreading going home, he dragged himself up off the hard bench. He would definitely have to be home before ten *tonight* - especially after what had happened - even though it was a million to one there would be no fighting between his Mam and Dad. But that was the trouble, he thought, you couldn't win: the good part about his Dad being sober, and trouble being less likely, was cancelled out by him always being dead nasty when he was sober. There was something to be said for him being drunk, he thought, at least he was more friendly and sociable when he was drunk.

Leaving the Hopey, it was pouring rain outside and he was only wearing a jersey. So, feeling fit and lively after sitting so long, he began to run all the way home, but he would have run anyway. He always ran home from the Hopey.

While he was running he felt like one of the cowboys out of the Saturday Matinee pictures, especially when he would slap his arse with one hand whilst holding the reins of the make-believe horse with the other. All the kids ran out of the Hopey like that on Saturday afternoons.

Arriving home, he was drenched but he was pleased to see his Mam sitting reading the *'Echo* and his Dad, cutting Thomas's hair with the old scissors.

Thomas looked really helpless sitting in the chair with no back on it, with an old shirt wrapped around his shoulders and his Dad puffing and panting, as he moved around him. It was lovely to see them sober and everything orderly. And even the fire was lit, for a change, making the house seem really homely.

"Where've you been?" said his Mam with a suspicious look. But his Dad didn't say a word, as if nothing had happened. He sensed that he felt guilty and was sorry for shouting those dirty things at him earlier on. His Dad hardly ever spoke when he knew he was in the wrong.

Proud of going to the pictures on his own, and on a Wednesday night too, without even asking anyone for his picture money, he replied, "Been to see Mario Lanza on the Hopey." But he was immediately sorry for opening his mouth. Thomas, his head bent down staring at the floor, frightened to move in case the rusty scissors snipped his neck, suddenly raised his head. "Where the fuckin'ell did you get the money from?" he cried indignantly. "I'm fuckin' working all week and I can't..."

"Shut up!" his Dad interrupted angrily. "I nearly nicked yer there with these bleedin' scissors." Thomas quickly lowered his head again, but Sheridan knew that they must all be thinking the same. "I went down the market", he lied, "and got some money off the women on the stalls for running on messages for them." His Mam, looking hurt, said, "Yiz never think of yer mother when yiz get all this money do yiz?" She seemed to be addressing all of them, even his Dad, and he momentarily felt guilty about not buying her anything out of the ten shillings, but then quickly changed his mind. She didn't have any sympathy for him, did she? he thought. She hadn't even said a kind word to him yet. He'd ran off hours ago crying his heart out. But instead of being glad to see him come home safe, all she could demand was, "Where've you been?" as if he had done something terribly wrong. Fuck her! he thought defiantly.

And that old puffed out bastard with the rusty scissors! And pudding-head sitting in the fuckin' chair with the stupid basin haircut! None of them fuckin' care about me, so why should I care about them?

His Dad was now nimbly moving around the chair, snipping away at Thomas's head, sweating and puffing and blowing hairs all around the kitchen, "These fuckin' scissors are under the arm", he suddenly cursed. "Wouldn't cut butter. I could do a good job, if I had proper fuckin' scissors."

"A bad tradesman always blames his tools", said his Mam with quiet contempt. Stopping what he was doing, he stood staring at her for a moment, before angrily crying out, "Who's fuckin' talking to you? What d'you know about barbering?" And before she could respond, he went on, "With proper tools, there's nothing to it. Best barber in the Nick, I was. Cos I had the proper fuckin' tools." Then suddenly turning to Sheridan, he hissed through clenched teeth, "Listen you, I'll break your fuckin' neck if I cop you cutting cardboard boxes with my scissors!"

"I haven't been cutting anything", he pleaded. Although he was telling the truth, he was willing to take the blame rather than cause any more trouble between them all.

"Just let me catch yer, that's all", he muttered.

Neither his Mam nor Thomas took his part. They all seemed to hate him. And, as if his Dad hadn't done enough to him earlier on, here he was once again picking on him. He wondered whether he'd ever be happy in this house. All they ever did, he thought, was pick on you and hurt you and belittle you. If it wasn't Thomas, it was his Dad. The only happiness you ever got was when you made it yourself. But even then, they weren't satisfied, they had to rob you of *that* as well. When was it ever going to stop?

"There's nothing left for yer Tea", said his Mam, unsympathetically. "There's a bit of salmon paste left over in the cupboard, make yerself a cup of tea and a butty with it."

At the moment, just when he needed her most, she didn't seem like his Mam. She seemed like the cruellest woman in the world. And what made it worse, was that he knew she was only acting this way in order to keep the peace with his Dad. Suddenly, like an erupting volcano, he felt an upsurge of anger and tears, which spilled uncontrollably out of him. "Fuck yiz! Fuck yiz! Fuck all of yer!" he cried out in wild desperation. "I don't want nothing off any of yiz!"

His face now burning with temper and hot tears, he violently slammed the door behind him and ran upstairs, sobbing his heart out.

In the bedroom he began punching in wild frustration at the old flock mattress, his tears soaking the dirty old pillow. And strangely enough, he wasn't a bit afraid of the dark.

Chapter Thirteen

On a Monday morning in July, a week before they broke up for the Summer Holidays, the boys and teachers of William Huskisson County Primary School had a very sad happening... or so they made it out to be, thought Sheridan. Sloppy Joe Flaherty got run over by a tramcar and was killed on his way to school. But, at Assembly the next morning, when the entire school were singing hymns and saying prayers for him, there were lots of kids quietly giggling and messing about just like they always did. And the older lads were still as busy as ever, passing cigarettes, dog-ends and matches to each other, as though nothing had happened.

He got so mad at one giggling lad in front that he punched him really hard in the back. But when he fell to the floor, one of the teachers hustled through the packed lines and grabbed Sheridan by the neck. "I saw that!" he roared with a mad look, and frogmarched him onto the stage. And Mr Wilkes was so angry at him for ruining what he called, "the dignity of the occasion", he gave him four heavy strokes of Black Bess there and then. But, determined not to show the severe pain, he defiantly walked back through the lines in the crowded hall, with a grim expression but proud that *he* at least had done something for Flaherty.

As for Wilksie and the teachers and all the kids, he thought hatefully, they were just a dirty big crowd of phonies. None of them had ever liked Flaherty when he was alive, and he reckoned that they were all really glad to be rid of him - especially the teachers. For when he was alive, they would never cease telling him how much of a disgrace he was to the school through always being smelly and scruffy and late every morning.

Mr Wilkes had announced there would be a collection to buy a wreath. And on the morning of Flaherty's funeral, although Mr Henry asked for ten volunteers to accompany the Headmaster to the church for the funeral service, only three boys put their hands up. It was Cricket this afternoon, which meant you were out in the schoolyard for about two hours in the sun, and nobody wanted to miss *that*. Sheridan was so disgusted, that he began pulling clenched fists and giving them all threatening looks while Mr Henry wasn't looking, so that before long, nearly every kid in the class had his hand raised.

There were so many volunteers now that the ten best-dressed ones were selected. But although he wasn't even among the best-dressed twenty, he was allowed to go because he had been the first to volunteer.

When the class returned after lunchtime, Mr Wilkes came in carrying a large wreath and called the ten volunteers to the front of the class. The wreath was massive and in the shape of a heavenly star, and although he hadn't seen many wreaths, Sheridan thought it was the most beautiful he had seen. Despite its size, it wasn't gaudy or cheap-looking. Perhaps, he thought, that was because all of its flowers were of the same kind and the same colour - scarlet red. And he knew, from the Nature

Study lessons, that they were roses. From now on, he silently vowed, red would always be his favourite colour, and roses would always be his favourite flower. He always had a favourite something: a favourite singer, a favourite film star, a favourite boxer. And, although he wasn't even interested in football, he had a favourite team, so why not a favourite colour and flower?

Propping up the wreath against the wastepaper basket in the corner of the classroom, Mr Wilkes told them all to file out, one by one, to see what the whole school's collection had bought. When it came to Sheridan's turn, he spotted a small white card with a black and gold border stuck among the dark green leaves. Curious, he bent down to read the scrawly writing on it, but had only managed to read, "With deepest sympathy, from the children and staff of...", when Mr Henry shouted over from his high desk, "Come on, Connolly! You're holding everyone up!" He felt humiliated and angry at him, for making an everyday thing, and cheapening what had been a very sad, respectful moment. How would that old bastard know what it felt like? he thought. He was another one who'd never liked Flaherty.

Sheridan had never been a close pal of Flaherty's. But in the church that afternoon, the sight of his small coffin laid out on a trestle in front of the altar, and the sound of everyone singing, *There Is A Green Hill Far Away* was altogether too much to take, and for the life of him he couldn't stop the tears slowly filling up. But, surrounded as he was by his classmates, he felt really embarrassed. What, he thought, would they think of the Cock crying his eyes out at scruffy Flaherty's funeral? He'd never be able to live it down. So, burying his head deeper in the hymn book, he slyly gave his eyes a quick wipe with his jersey sleeve.

Looking up again, he stared and stared at the coffin, concentrating hard, and wishing with all his might that the lid would suddenly open and Flaherty would come back to life and free him, and all these people in here, from this smothering sadness. But to his sorrow the lid never budged all through the service.

When it was finally over, the volunteers were marched outside by Mr Wilkes and made to stand to attention, like a guard of honour, down both sides of the pathway leading to the main road. Then, some big men, dressed in black suits, came slowly carrying the coffin out of the church. As they passed, Sheridan felt proud at being so near the coffin and not being afraid. He thought he might be scared, as he was scared of even the thought of corpses and coffins. But to his surprise he wasn't. Maybe, he pondered, it's because it's only poor Flaherty.

Some women among the crowd at the bottom of the pathway were sobbing. But the mournful sound was suddenly drowned by a big green tramcar, slowly trundling past the church making a terrible screeching, clanging noise. Sheridan glared at it full of hatred. It was one of those big ugly bastards that was the cause of all this sorrow, he thought angrily. Right now, there was nothing he hated more than tramcars. A fuckin' big ugly monster like that, he thought, and the Corporation had the cheek to call it a "Green *Goddess*"! It was crazy. A goddess was beautiful and kind and gentle, like an angel. Such a lovely thing would never have mangled poor Flaherty like that between the tramlines. It didn't make sense. *Goddess?* Goddess my fuckin' arse! Green *Monster*, more like it! He knew it was impossible, but he really wished the coppers could round up every Green Monster - as he would call them from now on - and drive them all to the scrapyards and smash them to smithereens. If they'd

187

let him, he'd willingly smash one to bits in the Metweld garage in their street.

As the tramcar trundled on down the hill, the funeral cortege slowly left for the cemetery in the other direction. And, as the guard of honour of kids gradually broke up, Sheridan gazed at the vanishing hearse, covered in flowers, until it was out of sight and whispered to himself through watery eyes, "I won't forget you, Flaherty."

The sun was now shining brightly and, although it was still only three o'clock, Mr Wilkes, before leaving himself, had told the volunteers that, instead of going back to school, they could all go home. Hearing this, they all went berserk with delight, yelling, "Hooray! Hooray!" Some of the women mourners still milling around outside the church, shouted at them to, "Have a bit of respect yer ignorant little bastards!" But they took no notice. And, when they finally departed in twos and threes, they were still singing and hooraying to each other, thrilled to be going home so early.

Sheridan, unlike the others who lived locally, lived about two miles away so he began walking down the steep hill in the same direction as the tram. And half-way down at the tram stop, who was standing there alone only Mr Wilkes. He felt shy and awkward, having to pass the Headmaster in the street like this. It was all right if there were a few of you, he thought. But on your own it was dead embarrassing. Right now, it seemed as if he and Mr Wilkes were the only two people in the world, and it felt so strange.

When he was in school, and among all the other kids, it was nothing: the Headmaster's presence never bothered him. Even being caned by him didn't embarrass you all that much. *In school* Mr Wilkes was just the Headmaster caning you. He was just kind of impersonal, a big shell of aloof authority with no personal life or feelings or anything. I mean, he thought, you could never imagine Mr Wilkes laughing or crying or feeling pain or shame or being embarrassed by anything. You never actually thought of him as being *human*. But now, right here and now, just standing there at the tram stop, there was a kind of separateness, and loneliness and even *weakness* about him. For the first time, he seemed just like an *ordinary* person.

Strangely enough, Mr Wilkes himself seemed to sense this feeling too, because when he spotted Sheridan approaching, his authority, composure and impersonality seemed to drain away from him, making him instead feel jittery and awkward. He seemed uncomfortable at being caught like this by one of his pupils, stripped of all his power and authority.

As Sheridan drew nearer, the Headmaster quickly turned away to look down the hill, pretending not to see him. At this moment, to him, he was nothing; just a man waiting at a tram stop; an anonymous and powerless nobody. It was like being the most important man in the army being caught without his uniform. Yet, without his "uniform" he seemed more of a *real* person than he ever seemed in school. Humble, nice, lonely, and more... *human*. It suddenly struck Sheridan that he'd caught, if only for a split second, the *vulnerability* of Mr Wilkes - even though he didn't know what vulnerable meant.

Trying to understand why he suddenly felt like this, it puzzled and disturbed him. Because what he felt was a huge feeling of *pity* for Mr Wilkes. It was crazy. There was no reason for it; no reason at all to feel even a little bit sorry for the Headmaster of all people! *He* was a grown-up; he always had new clothes; he never had holes in his shoes or socks; he could smoke; he could go in pubs: he always had money jingling in his pockets; he could go to the poshest picture houses anytime he liked; nobody ever insulted him or caned him; he was boss of the whole school... and he didn't even *have* a sad face! So why on earth should he feel sorry for him right now. He didn't know why, but he just did.

Passing the tram stop, he quietly said, "Goodnight, sir", and was immediately ashamed of himself for being just like the teacher's pets, who were always trying to suck up to the teachers. But he wasn't trying to suck up to Mr Wilkes. He'd said it partly to break the tension, but mostly because he felt sympathetic and wanted to show his respect. But he guessed the Headmaster would still class him as a crawler.

Still pretending to be unaware of his presence, and with an expression of slight confusion, Mr Wilkes replied with mock surprise, "Oh! Goodnight", as if to imply, "I don't know you boy, but 'Goodnight' anyway."

Sheridan was glad when he was out of the Headmaster's sight and free from that uncomfortable strange feeling of them being the only two people in the world. Cutting across the bombed site, he suddenly thought how silly he must have seemed saying, "Goodnight", when the sun was still cracking the flags. And how even sillier Mr Wilkes had been for saying "Goodnight" back to him.

Aimlessly meandering down across the vast, rubble-strewn, bombed site, he began, despite his Mam's repeated warnings, kicking a tin can, which had been lying in a pool of dirty water in the gutter. But as the soaking wet label gradually came off, he was reminded of what it was like going to school in the rain with leaking shoes and wet socks, so he quickly stopped. But still quite a way from home with nothing else to occupy him, he found himself thinking about Flaherty again, and how he would miss all the fun of the Summer Holidays and the Festival of Britain, and how he'd never be on the earth ever again. And when it dawned on him that, even if he lived to be a hundred, he'd never *ever* see Sloppy Joe again, in school or anywhere else, the horrible thought of it made him dizzy and panicky. But although the shock of this made him stop thinking about Flaherty, deep down he still felt really sad. So at the risk of the horrible feeling returning, he again whispered to himself, "I won't forget you, Flaherty lad."

After a while he decided he wasn't making much progress, so he pretended to saddle up his make-believe horse and started to gallop across the bombed site, smacking his behind with one hand, as he sang, "Wilksie is a dope, Wilksie is a dope, Ee-aye adio, Wilksie is a dope!" And in no time, he was turning the corner of their street.

Chapter Fourteen

The Summer Holidays that year were the happiest six weeks Sheridan had ever known. No matter what happened in the future, to him Nineteen Fifty-One would always be the happiest year of his life. What with all the free shows and exhibitions, and the bands and processions and celebrations of the Festival of Britain, you just couldn't help but enjoy yourself all the time.

In the third week they had a huge party in their street for all the kids and grown-ups. All the houses were decorated with red, white and blue paper flowers and bunting, and even the kerb stones were painted the same colours. Everywhere you looked there were Union Jacks, and the houses that had electricity had their front parlour windows and front doors all lit up with coloured fairy lights. Everybody was enjoying themselves so much, he felt it was like having Christmas in the middle of summer.

The street party went on through the day and night, and all the kids were allowed to stay up really late. The Tremarco family even brought their huge radiogram outside and were playing all the latest Mario Lanza, Frankie Laine and Guy Mitchell records, and Sheridan was thrilled to see his Mam and

Dad and Mr and Mrs Owens and all the grown-ups, singing and dancing in the street. There was ale everywhere. So much that Sheridan, Reggie and Freddy sneaked a quart bottle from the Tremarco's window sill and went around the back entry, where they swigged the lot and ended up half-drunk. But all the grown-ups were so drunk themselves that nobody noticed... or even missed the stolen ale.

Another good thing about the holidays was his Mam taking him to New Brighton on the ferry boat. It was so exciting and adventurous, because he'd never been that far in his life.

She'd taken his cousin Mona with them because, she said, she felt sorry for her.

Mona lived with his grandmother and she had no mother or sisters or brothers. And her dad, his Mam's brother, Uncle Paddy, had been put in a lunatic asylum after trying to cut his throat when his wife was killed.

His Mam took them on everything in the huge outside fairground: the Dodgems, the Big Waltzer, the Helter-Skelter, the Ghost Train, and even the motorboats on the Marine Lake. And she'd brought lots of sandwiches and cakes and lemonade, so that when they became tired and dizzy from all the rides, they had a picnic on the seashore.

The only thing that spoiled it for him was the way Mona kept moaning all the time. She was a year older than him, but the way she carried on, he thought, always looking for attention and everything, you'd have thought she was a little baby. He was glad when his Mam took her straight home as soon as they got off the boat. Ever after he always called her by the nickname "Mona-lot". There were so many things that happened during that six weeks. But to Sheridan, the best by far - better than all the rest - was that his big brother, Brendan, came home on leave from the army.

He would never forget the shock when he saw him. It was on a Saturday evening and so unexpected. Earlier in the day, he and Freddy had been to Woolton Woods to collect blackberries for their mams to make blackberry pies. They had called for Reggie beforehand, but he said he couldn't go as his dad was taking him downtown to buy him a new suit. Although he didn't say anything, Sheridan wondered, with a tinge of jealousy, why he had to have yet another new suit because he already had plenty of new clothes.

It was seven o'clock, but the sun was still shining when they got back from Woolton, carrying two large National Dried Milk tins full of ripe juicy blackberries, their fingers paining like hell through being pricked time and time again on the thorny bushes.

The front door was open, and as Sheridan went along the lobby, he sensed something strange in the air. He could hear grown-up voices and it sounded as if the kitchen was packed out. One voice, lower than the others, sounded strange and unfamiliar, yet familiar too, so that it excited and disturbed him at the same time. Although he couldn't pinpoint who it belonged to, he thought it must be someone friendly, and important too, because by this time on a Saturday night his Dad would usually have been out in the pub.

Opening the kitchen door, he could hardly see anything for the smoke and steam because his Mam was cooking and had a kettle and a pan boiling together on the stove. He spotted his Dad first, sitting at the table in his shirt sleeves, smoking. Even without looking at his face, which was red and partly swollen, he could tell by his manner that he'd been on the ale this afternoon. As she stood peeling carrots and onions for the Saturday night pan of soup, his Mam was coughing with the smoke, but nobody seemed concerned. And although he was searching with squinted eyes through the smoke and steam for the strange guest, Sheridan tried not to make his curiosity obvious.

Suddenly, he spotted the neat army battledress tunic hanging from a nail on the coal cupboard door and felt a stabbing pain in his stomach. But the pain wasn't like all the other times. Instead of the usual heavy dread and nausea, there was a feeling of surprise and delight. And in the place of sadness and misery, there was anticipation and joy when he finally realised it was Brendan. But there was shyness too. And when he finally brought himself to look into Brendan's eyes, he quickly looked away. It was stupid, he knew, to be feeling like this, but he was simply lost for words and was mad at himself for being so shy. Yet, fully aware of how ridiculous he must have seemed, he still pretended he hadn't seen his big brother. Instead, he shouted nervously, "Hey Mam, I got yer a load of blackberries!" But surely, he thought, he's going to twig that I've seen him. Yet perversely, he still would not, or could not, acknowledge Brendan's presence.

It was Brendan, sitting smoking in his army shirt and braces, who finally brought the situation to an end. "God blimey", he said quietly, "*he* hasn't half shot up, hasn't he?" Sheridan blushed, but still pretended not to notice him. And the longer he kept this up, the more stupid he felt.

They had all stopped talking now until Brendan finally jokingly teased, "How's the little soft lad keeping then?" He always used to tease him, he remembered. But there was something nice about the way he did it. It never hurt or wounded you like when other people, such as Thomas, did it. When Brendan teased you, he seemed somehow to be paying you a compliment and made you feel important. He wasn't nasty like everyone else. He seemed to make you feel that his teasing was because he liked you so much and was so interested in you.

Still blushing and finally forcing himself to give Brendan a quick glance, he replied with a faint, shy grin, "I'm alright." Then, spotting the bulging khaki canvas haversack leaning against the coal cupboard door, he cried, "Is that yours, Brenny?"

"Yeah", he replied, quickly adding there were no sweets or anything in it. But the way he said it, Sheridan could tell he was only kidding.

Their newly found rapport was suddenly broken by his Dad. "Eh, lad", he said sarcastically, "I thought you were a good reader?"

"So he is", said his Mam defensively. "What of it?"

"Well, it's as plain as a pikestaff, isn't it?" he said, pointing to the haversack. Sheridan now felt even more stupid when he saw Brendan's name and army number splashed across the side of the haversack in large white letters. He also realised that it was a stupid question to ask in the first place for, even without the name and number, it could hardly have been anybody else's. But he supposed people do stupid things, and say even dafter things, when they are shy and a bag of nerves.

Seeming like years ago since he'd last seen Brendan, he quickly tried to reckon just how long it was, but he was too excited to concentrate properly. All he could remember was that he'd been in Junior 1 at school when he'd gone away, and now he would be in Junior 5 when he returned after the Summer Holidays.

Brendan was now talking to his Dad again and Sheridan at first felt jealous, but then quickly realised that it was better like this, because he could now stare at Brendan without feeling shy and without him even noticing. Through the smoke and steam of the kitchen, it immediately struck him how sun-burned his brother's face was. And although he didn't like admitting it, he was disappointed that he didn't seem as handsome as he'd been before he went away. And those tiny wrinkles around his eyes, especially when he smiled: they hadn't been there before. The sun mustn't half be hot in Egypt, he thought. And when Brendan got up to get something out of his haversack, he was shocked to see how smaller and sort of wiry he had become. In many ways it didn't seem to be the same Brendan. But at least, he thought thankfully, even this new Brendan would still protect him from Thomas and his bullying. Deep down though, he was sad about him changing so much. If he had his way, nothing or nobody would ever change.

Sitting down again with a bundle of photographs in his hand, Brendan was also holding something in his other hand. But he seemed to be trying to conceal whatever it was. Then suddenly, he casually drawled, "Here, there's some sweets for yer", as a big square tin of Butterscotch and several bars of chocolate came flying towards Sheridan, who eagerly grabbed them with both hands.

Brendan, he thought warmly, always acted the same as his Mam when he was giving you anything: just matter-of-fact, as though he didn't want any fuss or commotion made. And that seemed to make whatever they were giving you all the more enjoyable.

"Aw thanks, Bren", he cried. Then, because he couldn't think of anything else to say, he asked, "Where'd yer get these from?" With a mock expression of surprise, he lightly replied, "Found them in the desert. Where d'yer think, soft lad?" He knew it was another stupid question. But the novelty of his big brother sitting there, after being so long away, was making him so nervous and happy and excited that he didn't know what he was saying half the time. But now sitting on the hard backless chair, eating one of the chocolate bars, his shyness was gradually subsiding. And even though Brendan caught him several times, he kept staring at him in wonderment, still not quite believing he was home at last.

His Mam, having put the soup on, now sat down and asked to see the black and white photographs after his Dad. As he handed over another photo, Brendan said, modestly, "That's me messing around with the machine gun on manoeuvres in Port Said."

"Let's see, Bren", said Sheridan excitedly. But his Dad, peering over the top of his broken glasses, said, "What d'you wanna see for? You should be out playin'."

"Yeah, go on", echoed his Mam, as if she'd only just thought about it, "go out and play."

As he reluctantly left the kitchen, Brendan was still handing photos to his Dad, who in turn was passing them to his Mam. And just as he began to think the worst of Brendan for not sticking up for him, he heard him calling, "Eh Sheah, here a minute, I want yer." Dashing back along the lobby he was thrilled to bits to see him pulling out two half-crowns. "Here", he said with a deadpan expression, "go and buy yerself a yo-yo." The remark was meant to be funny but as usual he said it without any trace of a smile. Even when he had you in stitches, he always kept a straight face, thought Sheridan. He never seemed to realise just how funny he was. With a gasp of excitement, he shouted, "Aw thanks, Brenny!" and dashed out again, this time much happier.

It was going to be really great having Brendan home again, he thought. There would definitely be no trouble in the house while *he* was home. He'd even be able to go to the Hopey tonight without even once having to worry about his Dad and Mam fighting. And *that* Thomas! he thought happily, what a shock he was going to get when he came home and found Brendan sitting there!

Seeing Reggie in the street absently kicking a tin can along the gutter, Sheridan just couldn't contain his feeling of joy. "Guess who's come home today?" he cried excitedly. But Reggie wasn't a bit excited as he briefly looked up and said lazily, "I know. I seen him before you did. I seen him getting out of the taxi this afternoon."

Momentarily stuck for words, he was annoyed that his friend had seen Brendan arrive before him - especially the way he said it, as though he were bragging. Reggie didn't half think he was clever, he could be a real smart alec sometimes. But anyway, he thought, no matter if he did see him first, Brenny's still my brother, not his. He's only jealous because he hasn't got a big brother in the army who's come all the way home from Egypt. Because of Reggie's attitude, he didn't ask, as he usually did, if he was going to the Hopey. Instead, feeling secure with the two half-crowns in his trouser pocket, he bragged, "I'm going the Hopey tonight." Hearing this, Reggie's manner suddenly changed. "Are yer?" he cried. "What's on?"

"Aw, it's a smashing picture called *Showboat*", he replied teasingly. "Our Thomas saw it on the *Palais-de-Luxe*. It's in Technicolor as well."

"What's it about? Is it a war picture?"

Already peeved at his superior attitude, Sheridan now saw a chance to even up the score. "No, yer fuckin' dope", he replied, "it's all about singing and dancing."

"Aw, don't think I'll go then", said Reggie. "Don't like them kind of pictures."

Disappointed at the prospect of having to go alone, and knowing cowboy films were his favourite, he said coaxingly, "There's *a few* coweys in it though." Reggie fell for the lie. And, because he knew it would be easy getting in the Hopey through Sheridan knowing the doorman's secret, he said he would ask his mam for his picture money.

Then to make certain he asked, "Are yer sure there's coweys in it? It doesn't sound like a cowboy picture to me."

"Course it is", he replied trying to convince him. "It's all about coweys by a river. There's just a little bit of singing in it like, but only like when Roy Rogers and Gene Autrey sing that's all."

Finally convinced, Reggie nodded his agreement then showing interest in Brendan's homecoming, asked, "Did he bring anything home for yer?"

"I don't know yet. But he probably has because his haversack is packed out with things. He's already give me five bob." But Reggie sneered, "I bet yer he hasn't brought yer *anything*."

"How do you know?" Sheridan sneered back, "He's not a fuckin' miser yer know, like your dad." Now sulking, Reggie said quietly, "Well, me dad bought me new trousers and shoes today from downtown. More than what yours did."

Although feeling he had to coax him and handle him delicately, Sheridan had been getting more and more irritated with Reggie. But now he suddenly decided to show him he no longer cared whether he came to the Hopey or not. "Oh, did he now", he said, mimicking his smug tone. "Anyway, yer can go the fuckin' Hopey on yer own, I'm gonna go with Freddy Owens now." Then completely losing his patience, he added,

"And if yer wanna know, there's no fuckin' coweys in it. So it just shows how fuckin' thick you are."

Showing no reaction, Reggie continued to kick the tin can in the gutter as if that were a thousand times more important than the insults, whilst Sheridan, angry and frustrated at his silence, finally stomped away up the street to Freddy Owens's house.

On the way he glanced back to see Reggie still kicking the can, and suddenly felt sorry about what had happened. Because, despite him always showing off and trying to be better than you all the time, he still thought a lot of him. That's why he was his best mate. But although he wished he could go back and make friends with him, he knew it was a waste of time even wishing. To him, if you were the first to stick out your little finger to make friends that meant you had been in the wrong - and he hadn't been. It was Reggie who had started it. But even if he had been in the wrong he still couldn't have been the first to make friends. He was too proud and stubborn over anything like that.

After he had shouted several times through the letter box, Freddy's mam finally opened the front door. Sheridan liked her: she wasn't a miserable sourface like Reggie's mam, she was kind and always said hello to him when she saw him in the street or at the shops. "Is Freddy in, Mrs Owens?" he asked. "No, luv", she replied. "He's gone to stay in his Auntie Hilda's for the weekend."

"Oh, okay", he said, trying to hide his disappointment, but noticing, again, how big her belly *now* was. And as he strolled away, he again thought about her doing *it* with Freddy's dad.

Sheridan quietly cursed Freddy for letting him down - especially now when he was trying to be so independent of

Reggie. And thinking of Reggie made him feel even sorrier, but not out of pity for him like before. This time it was more regret and anger at himself for losing his temper so quickly and ending up with nobody to go to the Hopey with.

Walking back down the street, he was now more miserable than angry as the happy prospect of the Hopey gradually faded. He really wanted to see *Showboat* - mainly because Kathryn Grayson was in it – and he loved her. But he could never have enjoyed it on his own - not on a Saturday night.

After wrestling awhile with what to do or where to go, he thought, reluctantly, about saving his money and staying in tonight and once he'd finally made up his mind to do so, he began to feel a bit better. He knew, of course, there would be a certain price to pay when his Mam and Dad and Brendan went out to the pub. For a start, since he was staying in, his Mam would probably want him to take the ashes out, and do the hearth, and wash the dishes and tidy up. But, he thought optimistically, there was the good side as well. He'd be in charge of the whole house; he'd be able to mess around as much as he liked; he'd be able to do things like making pancakes with flour and water the way Thomas had shown him. He could also go rooting if he wanted, in the old Diddy Box, looking at all the old photographs and reading all the old papers and everything. Come to that, he had the money to buy candles with, so he could even go rooting upstairs in the rooms to see if his Mam had started planting things for Christmas, like packets of raisins and sultanas and tins of pears and peaches like she usually did. And what about Brendan's haversack? He could have a really good root through that!

The thought of all of these opportunities really brightened him up. Yes, he told himself, there were a thousand things you could do to pass the time without being lonely, when you were minding the house on a Saturday night - even if the wireless wasn't working.

Reggie, who had seen Sheridan leaving Freddy's, was still messing around with the tin can in the gutter and never even looked up as he passed. But, knowing he would be laughing to himself, Sheridan shouted over to him, "Well, me and Freddy are going to the Second House, see." But, finally raising his gaze from the tin can, he smugly said, "So what? I'm going in now to listen to *Dick Barton Special Agent* on the wireless." Sheridan was again totally eclipsed and stuck for an answer. Frustrated at not being able to ruffle him and so jealous of his working radio, all he could think to do was blow him a loud raspberry.

That was another thing so maddening about Reggie, he thought, you could never make him mad.

Chapter Fifteen

Entering the kitchen, everything seemed to Sheridan to be really dark and gloomy because of the thick clouds of cigarette smoke, and because nobody had bothered to light the gas mantle.

His Dad was stripped to the waist getting a wash in the enamel bowl in the corner alongside the cooker and making a terrible mess, splashing water everywhere and grunting and puffing as he swilled his face and neck.

Brendan was still sitting in the armchair in his shirt sleeves smoking, his khaki tie undone and his thick army braces hanging down.

Sheridan always enjoyed watching his Dad getting washed. It was like when he was eating tripe or pigs' feet: he always made even a simple thing like a wash seem so refreshing and appetising.

He guessed that maybe he made it seem so enjoyable because he was always so thorough: doing it properly, rinsing his neck and behind his ears. Or maybe it was because his face and neck were always so red that the whiteness of the soapy lather seemed so clean and tasty.

Because his Dad was so busily occupied with his back to them, it seemed as if he and Brendan were the only ones in the room. And because this made him feel shy again, instead of asking Brendan, he turned to his Dad and asked, "Hey Dad, where's me Mam gone?"

His Dad, who for some reason always shouted when he was getting a wash, roared back, "She's upstairs making the beds."

Looking sheepish, he slunk down in the armchair facing Brendan and grinned nervously at him. And, to let him know he shared his amusement, Brendan grinned back, but this brought on the shyness again, so he quickly looked away.

Then, with a serious expression which Sheridan could tell was put on, he asked, "Are you top of the class yet, soft lad?" Catching on to this light-hearted mood, he cheekily replied, "Course I am. I'm not a big dunce like you, yer know."

The amusement trickled out of Brendan's eyes now, but he still tried to hide it, as leaning forward in the chair, he exclaimed, "Ah little wise guy, eh? The little soft lad getting some brains at last!"

Then, pretending disbelief, he added, "Get away, yer little liar, If the truth was known, I bet you're bottom of the class." Unsure of whether Brendan actually believed this, he said, "No, honest to God, Bren I came second in the exams, before we broke up for the Summer Holidays." But, refusing to be serious, he still pretended to mock him. "Get away with yer", he jeered, "you couldn't even come second in a two man race. Okay then, clever arse" he said, "seeing as your so brainy, what's two and two?" With casual confidence, he replied, "That's easy. Four. Everybody knows that."

"Ah, that's where your wrong yer see", he said with a wise look. "Two and two is twenty-two."

Sheridan laughed, not so much at the trick question being especially funny, but at the sheer warmth and happiness exuding from his big brother.

"Ah, that's not fair", he said sourly but not feeling sour. "That's a trick, that is." But Brendan, with the twinkle still in his eye, persisted, "It's not, yer know. Two and two is twenty-two."

His Dad was now drying himself on an old, torn, white shirt "Go 'head there Bren", he invited urgently, "muck in, get a quick swill. It'll liven yer up." Then to Sheridan he said, "Eh lad, go down and get a clean bowl of water for yer brother."

He was annoyed at his Dad breaking up the happy mood, but he wasn't surprised. He knew he never had any patience with jokes or anything when he was waiting to get out to the pub. It was too serious a matter. But he was only too pleased to do anything for Brendan, and because it wasn't yet dark, he willingly grabbed the bowl of dirty water.

On the way down to the cellar he heard his Mam upstairs in the back bedroom, moving the beds around. He was thrilled, because nowadays she never made the bed for him and Thomas, so it could only mean one thing: she was making up the hospital bed - the one they'd got off the Assistance Board a few months ago - for Brendan. Hooray! he thought, Brendan's gonna sleep in our room!

Just before they left, his Dad asked Brendan which pub he wanted to go to, He replied that he wasn't particular, "I'm just glad to be home. Wherever you and me Mam wanna go." With a thoughtful expression, his Dad then said, "Well, let's see, *Walker's* on the corner's no good, I'm barred. Can't get served in the *Threlfall's* either. The ale's no good in there anyway, and the manager's one prick and..."

Looking dis-heartened, Brendan said, "Don't tell me yer still getting barred out of all the alehouses. It's about time yer quietened down a bit and behaved yerself, isn't it?"

"I'll tell yer what", his Mam broke in, let's try the *Caledonia*, the little Higson's house. It's a lovely little pub that... some nice people get in there."

"Fair enough", said Brendan. "That okay with you, Dad?"

Still deliberating to himself, but anxious to get to the pub, he said with a sigh of resignation, "Yeah, ok. *I'm* game."

Then, as if suddenly remembering, he added, "Hope that fuckin' Wainwright fella isn't in there. Yer know, that window cleaner? Practically lives in there, he does. Always in the bar playing fuckin' darts and suckin' up to the barmaids. Mean bastard. Wouldn't give yer last year's fuckin' *'Echo*, the dying-looking cunt."

"What are yer worrying about people like that for?" said Brendan. "If yer don't like him, ignore him. Yer don't owe him anything, do yer? Gives yer nothing, does he?"

But, to his Dad that was precisely the problem: the window cleaner never ever offered him a drink.

His Mam too, was now becoming irritated. "Look", she said to both of them, "We're going out to have a nice happy drink." Then to his Dad, she said firmly, "Listen you, you're going out with yer son, we don't wanna know about your fuckin' alehouse cronies and bums." Aware he was outnumbered, his Dad didn't reply. And as they went down the lobby, Sheridan hoped they would enjoy themselves and have a really good time - if only for Brendan's sake.

Shortly afterwards, he placed the old flat iron against the front door to keep it open, and galloped around to

McDonough's to buy himself a quarter of caramels and a big bottle of Sarsaparilla.

His choice of Sarsaparilla instead of Tizer or Cream Soda, was deliberate because you could pretend it was ale - especially if you shook it well to give it a frothy head.

The light under the soup was turned off. He guessed it must have been cooked before they went out, so at least he wouldn't have to keep an eye on *that*. Looking around the kitchen, he was relieved to see it didn't need all that much cleaning up. He'd have it done in no time. As for the dishes: there were only a few dirty cups and plates to wash. But the thought of the cellar immediately made his stomach turn over. So, determined to act before the fear became too much, he lit a piece of screwed-up newspaper, grabbed the bowl and kettle and dashed downstairs.

On his return, he lit another piece of paper and climbed onto the table to light the gas mantle. And as the room gradually brightened, he congratulated himself on being brave, going down in the cellar like that. And funnily enough, he thought, the slugs didn't seem to bother him as much as they used to.

Later, he surprised himself at how quickly he had tidied up and done the dishes. But when he began to cautiously hide the knives and the glass vases, like he always did when he was expecting his Mam and Dad back drunk, he suddenly realised there was no need: Brendan was home now and he was sure his Dad wouldn't dare start anything in front of him. It felt really great not to be frightened for once, so with the few glass vases and bowls he could find, he tried to decorate the sideboard and mantelpiece.

For his rooting expedition, he decided it would be best to start with Brendan's haversack. If he left that to last, he might get caught in the act when they came back. He'd rather get caught rooting in the old Diddy Box than Brendan's luggage.

The white circular cord at the top was tightly looped through metal-ringed holes, but he managed to loosen it enough to start extracting the things nearest the top. He was disappointed though, because there was only the wet towel he'd got dried with and some army shirts and boot polish and shaving gear. There were no more sweets or presents or anything nice like that - not at the top anyway. But before going any further, he opened up the large orange polishing duster and, seeing the can of Brasso Brendan did his brasses with, and the tin of Blanco he used on his belt and lanyard, he couldn't resist raising them to his nose and taking a deep sniff. He really loved that clean, grown-up, army smell.

Suddenly, his face flushed and he felt a wave of panic sweep over him. But it wasn't caused by the fear of being caught by someone unexpectedly coming in. It was because he was suddenly aware of his crazy behaviour.

Other kids, he thought, like his mates or anyone like that, wouldn't even dream doing stupid things like smelling rags and polish. The feeling was so frightening and strange that for one horrible moment, he thought he might be going mad, so he quickly put everything back in the haversack and re-tied the cord.

He later thought that the terrible sensation he'd experienced must have been God's, or somebody's, way of paying him back for being so nosey and disrespectful, especially towards Brendan, who never seemed to think bad of anyone. Feeling horribly guilty, he whispered to himself, "Serves you fuckin' right, yer sly bastard."

His self-disgust reminded him of the time Mr Wilkes had made a speech one morning in Assembly, when he'd said that if you did anything good you'd always feel good, but if you did anything bad, you'd always feel bad afterwards. At the time he'd thought anything like that was impossible. It was just like saying if you were clean in body and dress, your thoughts would always be clean, but if you were dirty and scruffy you would always have filthy thoughts. He'd thought Mr Wilkes must either be dead stupid or else he thought *they all* were. But now, after what had just happened, he wasn't so sure anymore, and he didn't think he ever would be again.

The guilt he felt about invading Brendan's privacy didn't stop him from getting the old Diddy Box out of the coal cupboard. You didn't have to feel guilty or ashamed about rooting in this, he reassured himself, because you weren't poking into anyone's privacy. It had no lock on it, and, in any case, apart from himself, just about everybody in the house had had a good root in it at one time or another. It was a sort of ritual, a habit they all had, probably when they had nothing else to do, he thought. Or maybe they were just dead nosey, like him.

Taking out a well-worn wallet bulging with old photographs, he was about to go through them, when he spotted some old copies of the *Liverpool Evening Express* lying underneath. He somehow sensed that there must be something in them to do with their family. Otherwise, he thought, why would his Mam or Dad bother to keep them?

Laying them out on the bare kitchen table, he saw the first one was from January, Nineteen Forty-Eight. It carried big headlines about someone called Gandhi, who had been assassinated. Alongside was a photograph of his body being burned in India in front of thousands of people. Thinking that this Gandhi, whoever he was, must have been somebody really important, he started reading the article, but after learning that getting burned on a funeral pyre was the custom in India, he soon lost interest. His eye then caught a smaller headline further down the page which said, *"Blitz Hero Gaoled For Assault"*.

He'd heard a lot about the Blitz through listening to his Mam and Freddy Owen's mother chatting about it; about the people they knew who had been killed and things like that. But what he now read was totally unexpected. For the "Blitz Hero" was none other than his Dad. He'd never heard his Mam or Mrs Owens, or anybody, mention *this* before. The sudden revelation made him flush and caused a fluttering in his chest, and as he read further, he became even more excited:

"Former merchant seaman, Francis Joseph Connolly, who was awarded the George Medal in 1942 for rescuing a family of four from their blazing home during the May Blitz of 1941, was gaoled for 18 months today at Liverpool Assizes. He had been found guilty of wounding his wife, Catherine Connolly, of the same address, with intent to do grievous bodily harm…"

At first he was stunned, then overcome with shame and embarrassment, as he rapidly ran through a list of all the people who must have read this, without him knowing a thing about it. There must have been hundreds, he thought hopelessly. Mr Henry and Mr Wilkes for a start, and that Miss Jones out of the Infants. I bet that's why she hated me? They must've all read it, he winced. And what about the neighbours in the street, and Reggie's mam? Was that why she was always so horrible to him? Yeah, it all fitted together now. That must be why she always kept the front door locked, whenever he called for Reggie.

One thing which puzzled him was not remembering his Dad being sent to gaol for such a long time. After all, he'd been seven and a half in January, Nineteen Forty-Eight, and he could remember things from way before that, even from when he was three or four.

Slowly and carefully, he thought back. Forty-Eight, Forty-Eight, Forty-Eight... Ah! Yeah, now I remember! Yeah, that must have been the time me and Thomas were sent to me Nanny's in Scotland Road. Yeah, it all fits in now, he thought. Me Mam telling us how me Dad had gone on a long trip, and of how glad she was because he'd at last got a ship and had started going away to sea again, after being months on the Dole.

Feeling wise beyond his years, he thought, just goes to show how the grown-ups kid you when you're a kid. They must think kids are really thick. Then, realising that Thomas, and certainly Brendan, must have known all about it, he began to feel really annoyed with all of them for keeping him in the dark all this time. They could have told me, he thought. I mean, they could have told me by now, after all this time, couldn't they?

Still smarting at being deceived, he began reading where he'd left off:

"...In a plea for leniency, Mr Trevor Lloyd-Rees K.C. told the court that since the rescue of Mrs Silvano and her children from their bombed and blazing home in 1941, Connolly had suffered some injuries and severe mental stress, which caused him to drink excessively. It was in one of these drunken bouts that he had lost control of his temper. Connolly, said Mr Lloyd-Rees, could not recollect the attack on his wife, but in view of the jury's verdict, he wished to express his profound regret. He asked the court to consider these factors before passing sentence. But Mr Justice Grenville told Connolly, of Olivia Street, Liverpool 8, "You have been rightly convicted of a wicked and cowardly assault. Your wife's injuries necessitated no less than fifteen stitches. You are exceptionally fortunate in having a wife who is willing to stand by you, despite your contemptible act. I cannot, however, allow such violent behaviour to reign unchecked. I take full cognisance of your

past heroism. Indeed, but for this, the sentence I pass on you would have been much more severe. You will go to prison for eighteen months."

As he read the newspaper report over and over again, the initial shock and shame was gradually replaced by a feeling of pride. But not because of his Dad winning the George Medal - although that had been a real surprise. And he certainly wasn't proud of his terrible attack on his Mam - especially when he thought of all those people who must have read about it. No, strangely what made him so proud, was their name and their address being in the newspapers! He'd never thought their house, or anyone in it, had ever been, or ever would be that important. Yet he couldn't really enjoy feeling proud, because deep down he sensed it was wrong. But he still didn't feel wholly ashamed, just kind of queer and guilty.

Spreading out another copy of the *Evening Express*, he saw on the front page a photograph of a group of soldiers standing on a hill with their arms around each other's shoulders. They were all stripped to the waist and smiling, and the caption underneath simply said, *"Wish You Were Here"*. And, as he scrutinised each face, he was thrilled to see Brendan's, right there in the centre of the photograph, wearing a big smile from ear to ear.

The group was called the "Liverpool Kingsmen", and Brendan's name was there among the other names. It said they were enjoying a spot of off-duty sun in the Canal Zone. This time he felt *truly* proud without anything spoiling it. Fancy our Brendan being famous in the papers eh, he thought. It was smashing! Just shows you, doesn't it. Brendan's photo and everything, in the *Evening Express*! It was unbelievable.

Folding the newspapers and carefully replacing them in the Diddy Box, he was annoyed that nobody had told him anything about all these things that had happened in his family. But he was even more annoyed with himself for not taking the trouble to read the papers more often and more carefully. If he'd done so, he thought, instead of gallivanting the streets or sitting in the Hopey, nobody would have had to tell him.

He was fascinated, and itchy with curiosity about his Dad winning the George Medal. But, he thought, if he asked anybody about it, they'd know immediately that he'd been rooting in the old box and he'd probably get a smack for being so nosey. Not that the actual smack would worry him, he'd had plenty of those. What was more worrying, was the wretched humiliation when you were found out doing something you weren't supposed to, and everyone started picking on you and lecturing you. He couldn't stand that. It made you feel as small as anything, he thought.

He'd put the box back in the cupboard now and was standing in front of the large sideboard mirror, swigging away at the bottle of Sarsaparilla, pretending he was a drunken cowboy. It had become a bottle of whisky and he was in a saloon in the Wild West like in the cowboy pictures. And every time he took another swig, he shook the bottle to make it more fizzy and frothy, to imagine himself drunker - although the whisky in the cowboy pictures was never as frothy as his Sarsaparilla.

To make his actions even more authentic, he messed up his hair and slowly began undoing the three buttons on his jersey. And when the performance was in full swing, and he was supposed to be paralytically drunk, his eyes began to sag as he let the Sarsaparilla seep out of the side of his mouth and down his chin.

By the time half the bottle had been drank, he was swaying on his feet and mumbling incoherently. And, still leering into the mirror, his facial expressions were going from lunatic grins and hysterical laughter to aggressive drunkenness. Then, strangely, his cowboy muttering began to come out in an authentic western accent, surprising even himself at how good his performance was. This self-congratulation encouraged him to fall even deeper into the part, as he exaggerated his actions, making his voice louder and making himself appear even more drunk and aggressive.

But always, throughout the whole act, he was constantly aware of a tiny part of him, an almost unconscious part of him, which stayed clear and "sober", which was observing his entire performance. He thought of it as the "audience" part of himself, a sort of "third eye".

Detached and critical throughout, it was almost unnoticeable, and although he tried, he just couldn't bring it into "the act". And without this part, he felt there was something missing, things were not *complete*. To him it was like the Hopey on a Saturday night without Old Lizzie. Or Al Jolson singing without his black face. Somehow it wasn't a hundred per cent. Yet, he realised that without this "audience" part of himself, he wouldn't have been able to enjoy his performance. The terrifying thought then occurred to him that, without this detached "third eye", tiny as it was, he wouldn't simply be pretending to be a drunken cowboy, he might have, or even *would* have actually become one! Then, someone else, and then someone else again. It would be out of control. It would be like being lost in space on your own forever and ever, and you'd never know anything again for real. You'd never even know *who* you were anymore.

He'd had a taste of how horrible this would be, a few months ago, when he'd been in the house alone, just like tonight. He'd got the wet dish towel and covered his face with soot from the fireplace. Then, putting on his black Sunday blazer over his white vest, he'd stood singing in front of the mirror for so long, pretending to be Al Jolson, that the mirror started playing tricks on him until finally, the black-faced, gruff-voiced person in the mirror seemed like somebody else altogether. He seemed to become unrecognisable: taller and older, and more, more... alien. He'd become so scared that night at the weirdness of it all, that he quickly tore off the blazer and vest in a panic and frantically scrubbed the soot off his face with the wet flannel. And it was only when he again saw his normal self in the mirror, that he thanked God he was back to the safety and security and warmth of normality and ordinariness.

Still pulling faces at himself in the mirror, he suddenly heard *Bless 'Em All* at the front door. He hadn't expected Thomas home so early. Feeling panicky, but trying to keep cool, he quickly put the top back on the bottle and hid it behind the sideboard, before dashing along the lobby.

As he led the way back, he couldn't resist shouting over his shoulder, "Guess who's home? Our Brendan."

But Thomas, pretending to be unimpressed and doing his utmost to appear grown-up, chidingly said, "Alright, alright, stupid arse, keep yer shirt on, no need to start flapping." Then, trying to conceal his curiosity, he casually asked, "When did he come home?"

Sheridan was not only proud to be first with the news to *somebody,* but also reckoned that, as the carrier of some good news, Thomas would be nicer to him. But when he excitedly told him Brendan had been home since that afternoon and was now in the pub with his Mam and Dad, neither his face nor his attitude changed. He was still as miserable as ever, and still as nasty to him. He'd been to the *Majestic* - to see a John Wayne film as usual, But, he thought, this time, Thomas's hero must have been killed, at last!

Chapter Sixteen

When Brendan and his Mam and Dad arrived back from the pub, they were laughing and singing and joking and loaded up with quart bottles of ale.

Sheridan could see that his Mam and Dad were pleased as punch to have Brendan home, and that he was just as happy to be home. For once there was no nastiness from his Mam towards his Dad and everybody seemed truly happy. And after being coaxed by Brendan to help himself to the ale, even Thomas joined in.

Wherever Brendan was, thought Sheridan warmly, there was always enjoyment and happiness. It must be something special about him. It couldn't just be coincidence that this was the happiest Saturday night he could remember in years.

Although he'd had several cupfuls of ale, Sheridan, although tipsy, wasn't drunk. But he was so eager to become part of the happy atmosphere, he didn't hesitate when his Dad asked him to sing. And by way of welcoming his big brother home, he decided to sing *Among My Souvenirs*: not only because Brendan always used to sing it, but because it was one of the few songs he knew all the words to.

When he finished, they all clapped him. But what pleased him most was seeing Thomas clapping and, for the first time in ages, smiling at him with pride and brotherly love.

Seeming to catch an inkling of this, his Dad, who had been playing an imaginary piano on the bare kitchen table, suddenly stood up and drew the three of them to him. And after giving each a hearty hug, he clasped their hands in each other's in a family bond and proudly sighed, "Ah, my sons, my lovely sons."

Trying to ignore the sentimentality of the occasion, Thomas smiled bashfully, as Brendan shook his hand in manly fashion. And Sheridan, although loving every minute of it, lowered his gaze in embarrassment. If he really let this atmosphere get a hold on him, he was afraid he would burst into tears of sheer happiness and probably make a laughing stock of himself.

It was one o'clock before Sheridan went to bed. As he said goodnight his Dad, who seemed to have sobered up a lot, was sitting in the armchair reciting to Brendan and Thomas, who were laughing their heads off, a bawdy ditty called, *The Grand Farting Contest*. But he was glad to get away, because it was so coarse and embarrassing. His Mam had long since gone to bed. But before she went, she made sure they all emptied the big pan of soup. She always said it was, "the best thing in the world for you after a bellyful of ale." She even gave it credit for her never having a hangover.

When Brendan first came home, he always seemed to Sheridan to have plenty of money and loads of cigarettes - big cartons of them, which he said were dead cheap in Egypt. And he'd always be in the pubs every night, or in one of the posh picture houses downtown. But after about a week he noticed a big change: Brendan was broke. He could tell, because now all he ever did of an evening was stand for hours on the street corner with a few of his mates who were also on leave from the army or navy.

When he would be playing in the street with Reggie and Freddy, he'd often see Brendan asking one of his mates for "afters" of his cigarette, and after a few puffs passing it on to somebody else. Seeing this sort of thing made him sad and embarrassed for his big brother, although Brendan, he thought, would never have suspected in a million years how he felt. It also hurt and shocked him to discover that Brendan could, at times, be just as nasty as Thomas.

The first sign of this was on a Monday night, when he and Freddy Owens were playing near the corner of the street, and Brendan and his mates were whistling up the main road after some girls on their way to the skating at the roller rink.

They were playing Tick, and running around in circles around the big fellows when suddenly without warning, Sheridan felt a slap around the side of his face. It hurt and went all red, and when he looked up, he was shocked to see Brendan shouting at him to "fuck off" and go and play elsewhere. His face was stinging from the smack, but that didn't hurt him half as much as the disappointment and pain of Brendan, whom he loved and admired so much, turning on him like that.

Walking back down the street, he was nearly in tears; not for himself, but for Brendan because he seemed more pitiful than wicked. He guessed he was so miserable and narky, because he had no money and nothing to do and nowhere to go.

In certain ways, Brendan was like himself. And he knew how he would have felt if, after being so well-off and important like him, he'd had to stand on the street corner every night, so skint that he had to cadge a drag of his mate's ciggy. Oh, he thought, Brendan would never let himself go down into the gutter; he was still as smart as ever, and he still kept his uniform and everything immaculate, and he never complained or seemed to feel ashamed or anything. But deep down, he sensed that his big brother, who seemed so proud of being a soldier, was really sad through having no money, and not being able to go to the dance hall or the pictures or the pub anymore. And - as smart and handsome as he was - not being able to get a girlfriend through never having anything. His Dad always said that, if they knew you were skint, girls didn't want to know you. They could afford to ignore the likes of Brendan, because they could take their pick of the Americans from Burtonwood - and *they* were loaded.

He didn't know exactly what the word "dignity" meant, but he still reckoned that a British soldier like Brendan shouldn't have to lose all his pride and suffer like that just because he hadn't enough money to see him through his leave. The army, he thought, should give them plenty of money when they were home, so they could enjoy themselves and afford to go anywhere they liked, so that girls wouldn't look down on them.

On the surface Brendan seemed content enough. But the more Sheridan sensed his situation, the more he felt sorry for him. It seemed to him that they only gave you a uniform and all that, just to kid you that you were a man, but that really they just treated you like a young kid. It reminded him of when his Dad would tell Thomas off and try to belittle him by saying, "When lads have money they think they're men, but when they're skint they're lads again." It was insulting, he thought. And the way the army treated soldiers like Brendan, they were no better than his Dad. But then again, in fairness to his Dad, he recalled the little song he always sang to them: *Put A Little Bit Away For A Rainy Day*, and the words, *"Your best little friend is your pocket in the end, so always put a little bit away."*

Feeling miserable and helpless, he wished he had some money to give Brendan, but then realised it would be just as shaming and pitiful for him to have to accept help from his kid brother. He desperately needed to look up to him, but he was finding it harder with each passing day. All the glamour surrounding his big brother when he'd first arrived home seemed to have slowly seeped away now.

The saddest part of all was one evening when he saw him standing on the corner with his mates, skint as usual, and found himself actually wishing he would go back to Egypt or the Canal Zone or wherever it was. He shocked himself that night, because he never thought he would ever wish something like that about Brendan of all people. But at least, he thought, he would have money again and his pride back, and he would still be able to be proud of him, and he'd still have something to look forward to when he came home on leave again. He didn't know why, but he always felt that was one of the most important things in the world - having something to look forward to.

The only thing that stayed enjoyable about Brendan, was watching him spend hours every night pressing his uniform with the old flat iron and a sheet of brown paper, and polishing his brasses and boots, and Blanco-ing his belt and lanyard. When he was in a hurry to go out, he would let Sheridan polish his boots or Blanco his belt and lanyard. It pleased him that he was able to be of some help in some way to his big brother, and he felt really grown-up as he sat spitting assiduously on each boot in turn and rubbing the polish around the toecaps in little circles until they were so shiny, he could see his face in them.

Brendan always took so much pain over his uniform, he thought, you would think he was going on guard at Buckingham Palace or somewhere, instead of just going out to stand on the stinking corner all night, smoking dog-ends and whistling after hard-faced, scruffy girls.

The weeks went by and Brendan was still home, still lounging around on the corner of the street every night. But Sheridan noticed his appearance was becoming scruffier, and he hardly ever wore his uniform or anymore. That puzzled him for a while until he realised why, or thought he did.

He had heard his Dad one night telling Brendan that he was "fucking stupid" to have joined the army; that he was just something called "cannon-fodder" and that he would be sent to Korea where there was a war on and he might get his head blown off. Brendan had told him not to be silly, that people just don't get killed every day. He knew there was a war in Korea, he'd said, but he was in the army, and if he was sent there, then that was what the army was for. There were thousands of soldiers in the army and the chances of being killed were one in a million.

But Sheridan guessed Brendan must have had second thoughts about what his Dad had said because, being home on leave for so long, and allowing himself to become so scruffy, meant only one thing: he'd decided not to go back, and was now on the run. He was even more certain of this when, one evening on the street corner, he saw Brendan and his mates scatter when they saw two policemen walking up the main road towards them. It was only when he went back to the army that Sheridan discovered he hadn't gone on the run because of what his Dad had said, but because he'd fallen in love with a girl named Jean McShane from a few streets away.

Brendan's four weeks on the run was an horrendous time for Sheridan. Almost every night, when Brendan and his Mam and Dad were talking in the kitchen, he had to stand by the front door or sit on the cold steps for hours on the lookout for police cars or the military police ambulance. His Dad had told him to keep douse for an army ambulance with a big red cross on it, because Brendan was supposed to be sick. He also told him that it wasn't really an ambulance, and that they only sent that to drag you back into the army, that instead of nurses it was driven by "Red Caps" who were military police, and once they got you inside the ambulance they punched and kicked you all over the place for going on the run.

Sometimes he would be on watch from six o'clock in the evening, till eleven or even midnight, and to pass the time he would often look up the street and gaze at the illuminated lamp over the door of the *Walker's* pub on the corner. It was an unusual lamp, he thought, because it was square instead of round like most lamps. And on the four sides were the head and shoulders of a huntsman in red tunic and black hunting cap, which was the brewery's trademark. On a cold, misty night it gave out such a warm, cosy glow, and was so colourful in the surrounding darkness, that it seemed to give out a promise of something better to come in his life. It became a shining beacon of anticipation, of adventure, of happiness and security, of something to look forward to. And although he'd stare at it for so long and so intensely that it sometimes became blurred or the head would seem to move or he began to see a double image, it always gave him a warm feeling of reassurance that things weren't so bad, and that everything would turn out all right in the end for Brendan and his family and himself.

The night they caught Brendan, Sheridan was on lookout at the front door as usual, when, at about ten o'clock, a scruffy-looking black saloon drove slowly down the street. Two men, wearing trilbies, were sitting in the front. And as it cruised past, the driver stared at him for several seconds in a curious, rather than a menacing, fashion. Equally curious, he watched until the car slowly turned the corner at the bottom of the street.

Although he'd never seen the men before, and although not many cars usually came down their street, he thought no more about it. But several minutes later, he was horrified to see the same car racing back up the street and screeching to a halt in front of him. This time there were another two men in the back.

Before, he could collect his wits and warn Brendan or his Dad, the four of them were out of the car, two of them running up the back entry and two rushing past him up the lobby.

Brendan hadn't stood a chance, he thought hopelessly. He never even had time to jump out of the kitchen window into the backyard and get away down the entry. And even if he had, the other two men would have been there waiting for him anyway.

When they took Brendan away, his Dad called Sheridan all the stupid bastards under the sun for not alerting them. Why hadn't he realised they were detectives? he demanded. Didn't he know the "jacks" always drove black cars? He protested he'd only been told to look out for army ambulances or police cars, and didn't know the men were coppers. But deep down he felt as guilty as if he had deliberately betrayed his big brother. He should have been on his guard, he told himself. He should have twigged who they were, the sly bastards. After all, that's why he was keeping douse at the front door in the first place. He'd never seen the men before, and they did look suspicious, and cars hardly ever came down their street, especially at that time of night, so why, oh why, hadn't he caught on? His Dad was dead right. He was the cause of Brendan being caught. He *was* a stupid bastard!

Despite his guilt and shame, Sheridan tried to console himself about the brother he worshipped so much. Now that he was back in the army, he thought, Brendan would be kind of restored in his estimation, and he would be able to look up to him once more. But the conflicting feelings made him so mixed up and miserable that he cried for days afterwards whenever he was alone.

On a Saturday night, a few weeks after Brendan had gone, he was rooting among the pile of old letters and documents that were usually left on the mantelpiece, when he came across a letter from Brendan to his Mam and Dad. In it he told them he'd been confined to barracks for fourteen days and had had some pay docked. The good news, he said, was that next week their regiment was sailing from Southampton on the troopship *S.S. Devonshire*, first to Aden then Singapore and Hong Kong and then Korea. By the sound of the letter he seemed really excited, and looking forward to seeing all of those far-away places.

Since the night he'd discovered the old newspapers and read about his Dad getting put in gaol, and the George Medal business, Sheridan always made sure he read the papers thoroughly. So he knew about the war in Korea. But it didn't seem a proper war to him, not like when they'd had the Blitz and Hitler and Germans and everything. Of course, there was always something about it in the *'Echo* or the *Evening Express* every night. And sometimes there were names of soldiers who'd been wounded, or even killed, but it still didn't seem to be a real war. And because of this, he wasn't really worried about Brendan going out there. What worried him more was the part where he wrote that he would probably be away for two years. That was a hell of a long time to go before seeing Brendan again. But apart from that, he was, if anything, envious at how lucky his big brother was: sailing thousands of miles across the ocean on a real big ship like that, to such smashing, adventurous places like Hong Kong and Singapore. Just imagine being able to do that, he thought wistfully, instead of being stuck here every day in a lousy, stinking, schoolyard in dirty, scruffy Liverpool, looking at the same old teachers' pasty, fed-up faces, and having to put up with the same stupid lessons, day in and day out.

At times like this, he would long so painfully to be grown-up that he would actually feel an ache in his chest. It was the freedom more than anything else which made being grown-up so great. Maybe, he thought, that's what made Brendan seem so attractive - freedom. Apart, that is, from the times when he was skint on the street corner.

Chapter Seventeen

When they returned to school after the Summer Holidays, Sheridan went up two classes to Junior 6, the top class of the Juniors. Exactly why, he didn't know, but he guessed it was because they must have thought he was extra clever. Either that, he thought, or Mr Henry couldn't get rid of him quick enough. Whatever the reason, he was thrilled to bits, because in Junior 6 you were allowed, for the first time, to go once a week to Sefton Park for Games. But although it was great to get out of the classroom and away from the school for an afternoon, he wasn't all that keen on Games. He was hopeless at football, and that's all they ever played. Except in the summer when they played cricket, and, at that, he was even more hopeless.

When he first saw their new teacher, Mr Usher, he thought he looked a real bastard. With his scrawny body, his rimless glasses, his cruel thin lips and his over-sized head covered in a few long, thin wisps of fair hair, he reminded him of a German. But, when he got to know him better, Mr Usher turned out to be one of the best teachers he'd ever had, and what's more, like himself, he loved music.

One Wednesday afternoon during the Music lesson, he picked Sheridan for the school choir. This was going to be part of the massive Liverpool Schools Choir, which would appear at the *Philharmonic Hall*, as part of the city's "Festival of Youth" celebrations. Sheridan was thrilled to be chosen, and eagerly looked forward to Wednesdays, when he and ten other lads would spend almost the whole afternoon in the school hall rehearsing such wonderful songs as, *Greensleeves*, *Annie Laurie*, *The Mermaid*, and *The Lincolnshire Poacher*.

He knew that Mr Usher must have thought he had a good voice, because on this particular Wednesday, when he was playing *The Ash Grove* on the piano, he asked him to come and stand on the stage at the front of the whole choir and sing it. But, feeling terribly uncomfortable, he began to blush, and to hide his shyness, he lied that he had a sore throat, and Mr Usher never pushed him like some teachers would have done. Still, he thought proudly, it was a really big honour to be picked to sing at the *Philharmonic Hall* - even if there were going to be another hundred and ninety-nine kids singing with you.

It was a very busy time in school, because, he not only had the choir practice for three months, but it was also the year that you sat for the Scholarship if you were clever enough.

Only those who had been placed in the top ten of the class exams were allowed to sit it. And, always being among the class's top three, he was eligible, but he didn't like the idea of becoming a silly "college pudding". The thought of himself, the Cock of the Class, becoming one of those posh little cissies and having to wear the little black blazer and flannels and stupid little cap, horrified him. The mere thought of it was ridiculous. It wouldn't have seemed at all right. Yet, in spite of this, he knew his Mam and Dad would be really pleased if he could win the Scholarship and go to college. And, he had to admit, it would be smashing to shock all those well-off teacher's pets, who thought that they were brainier than you, just because they were always better dressed, and came from a better home, and never got the cane for being late. It would be worth winning the Scholarship, he thought defiantly, just to really fuck them up.

As well as appreciating his singing, Mr Usher also liked Sheridan a lot. He didn't quite know why. But ever since he'd read about his Dad in the newspaper, he always put whether a grown-up liked him or not down to one of two things: if they liked him, it was because they admired his Dad for winning the George Medal. But if they disliked him, it was because they thought his Dad must be one right bullying, vicious bastard. It made things a lot simpler to think that, if people hated you, it was, at the very most, only because of one thing.

What with the choir practice and preparing for the "eleven-plus" entrance examination - which was the posh name for the Scholarship - school was much more interesting, and the time seemed to fly so quickly that, before he knew it, the Scholarship exams were only two days away.

A great deal had happened since he'd come into Junior 6. The Festival of Youth had been wonderful. He'd felt really proud standing on the huge stage of the *Philharmonic*, with his clean white shirt and black tie on and wearing the new black shoes and grey stockings his Mam had bought him especially for the occasion.

He could clearly see his Mam in the seventh row, and the proud look on her face. The only thing that spoiled it was the empty seat where his Dad was supposed to be sitting. Why couldn't he have come? he thought, especially as he was supposed to like music and singing so much. But his Mam told him afterwards that as she was leaving, his Dad was getting a wash and said he was going to the alehouse.

That was the difference between his Mam and Dad, he thought. If she was proud of you, she was also proud of being proud. But his Dad? He always seemed bashful and ashamed whenever you did things that normal people do, things that he should have been happy and proud about. Either that, or he was just too fond of the ale. Still, he thought, at least me Mam saw me singing at the *Philharmonic Hall*, and that is *something.*

Not long after the "choir business", as his Dad called it, Thomas went into the navy to do his National Service. And although he'd always been like a miserable fog hanging over Sheridan for as long as he could remember, he'd nevertheless always been there. He'd never been away from home before, and it felt strange once he'd gone. The house seemed awfully empty now, and, in spite of everything, it wasn't long before Sheridan was wishing he was back home once again. It seemed as though his family, the only people he really loved, were gradually disintegrating. And the more he dwelt on it, the more sad it became, until he finally had to force himself not to think about it.

The realisation that he could miss somebody like Thomas - who had always been horrible to him - so much that he wanted to cry, frightened him. He didn't want to cry for Thomas. Why should he? He'd never done anything for him, never helped him, never been kind to him or anything. So why should he be so miserable just because he'd gone away? And if he was so affected by Thomas merely going away, it terrified him to think what it would be like if something happened to somebody he *really* thought a lot of: someone like his Mam or Brendan, or even his Dad. If anything happened to any of them, he was sure he'd never be able to stand it. And the thought that he must in some way be abnormal for thinking like this, frightened him anew. Other kids, he thought desperately, weren't like this, surely?

It wasn't only this feeling sorry for everybody all the time that was worrying him so much. What about the mirror? It was getting so that whenever he was alone in the house, he couldn't stop looking at himself, and pulling all kinds of weird faces, and pretending to be all kinds of different people, until he would become so dizzy and confused he wouldn't know *who* he was. And despite it causing him to eventually start panicking, he always went back to it. It was as if there was a magnet or some mysterious force inside the mirror, drawing him to it again and again. Sometimes he thought he might be going mad, because the more he looked into it, even though it sometimes terrified him, the more he wanted to be alone so that he could stare into it all the more. It was like being cheeky, he thought, or pulling tongues at the teacher or whistling in class, or some other dangerous things that you were certain to be punished for. But then again, it was even weirder than that. It was real scary, but also exciting in a funny sort of way.

Another reason for thinking that he might be going mad was his Dad's constant warnings about playing with yourself. He'd told him often enough, hadn't he? He recalled, his face flushing with embarrassment and anxiety at the very thought of it. How, apart from going blind and getting hairs all over your hands and losing all the hair on your head, you'd also become feeble-minded and turn into a lunatic. And, like with the mirror mania, he'd tried to stop but always ended up doing it.

That must be the reason why I can't stay away from the mirror, he thought, because I'm turning into a lunatic. He felt sure he would be a freak and a weakling when he grew up, yet strangely, he seemed to take a horrible delight in the knowledge and the certainty of it. And the more scared and hopeless he felt, the more he did it, which made him even more scared and hopeless and mad with himself. It was like being inside the Wall Of Death in the fairground, he thought: a kind of non-stop, never-ending, inescapeable feeling, that made you dizzy and terrified and sick and disgusted, yet still thrilled you.

One particular night, he decided to fight back. He didn't like the feeling of allowing himself to be dragged down the road to what he regarded as certain destruction, so he forced himself to stop doing it for several weeks. But instead of the guilt and terror being replaced by satisfaction and happiness, as he'd expected, he felt even less normal than before. So he started doing it again. And nothing, not even his terrible fear of growing up to be an imbecile, could stop him altogether.

He did finally stop though. It was the night before he was to sit for the Scholarship, and he never did it again for years. That was the night he'd always remember till the day he died. It was a nightmare, the most horrible gigantic nightmare he'd ever had. And what was so terrifying, was that he couldn't escape from it simply by waking up, because he was already awake. It was so unbelievable, that it was years later before he could accept that it had really happened.

It was Thursday, and instead of staying behind with Reggie and Freddy in Play Centre at school, he rushed home to tell his Mam that he was sitting for the Scholarship the next morning. Eager to tell her the news, because he felt so proud, he also wanted to tell her to get him up extra early because he had to travel all the way to a place called the Evered Technical Institute, which was so far away you had to get two buses. And because he didn't want to look scruffy and dirty, he had to have a shirt washed and his Sunday clothes ironed. But his excitement quickly turned to disappointment, because neither his Mam nor anyone else was in when he got home.

Looking in the oven, he saw a large plate covered by another. At least, he thought gratefully, she's left me my Tea. Ravenously hungry, he put the plates on the table, removed the top one and immediately began devouring the meal of mashed potatoes and stew and dumplings, pausing only to switch on the wireless. But there was only *Children's Hour* on, which he didn't like because it always seemed so silly and childish.

What he was waiting for was the serial, *Dick Barton Special Agent*: he really loved that, even though he hadn't been able to follow it every week because of the wireless sometimes not working. But now it was working almost all the time, because with Brendan, and now Thomas leaving her weekly money and not being there to eat any food, his Mam could afford to buy a battery whenever one was needed. And it only cost ninepence to get the accumulator charged in the Metweld garage across the street. So, with their reserve accumulator always on charge it meant, to his delight, that they never had to be without music and plays and programmes like *Ray's A Laugh*, *Variety Bandbox*, *Have A Go* and *Henry Hall's Guest Night*, and on Sundays, even *Family Favourites*.

His Dad didn't like the wireless. He'd told him once that a famous writer named George Bernard Shaw, had said it was for people who couldn't think for themselves. But during weeknights that didn't stop him listening to the news, because he reckoned the war in Korea was getting serious, and with Brendan being out there, he wanted to keep in touch with what was happening.

Finishing his Tea, he began to wonder where his Mam and Dad could be at this early hour. It was unusual for his Mam to be out when he came home from school, even on a Friday, much less a Thursday. And, even though his Dad was sometimes out early on Thursdays to catch all the navvies and dockers coming home from work on their pay day, it was more the exception than the rule.

For a second, he had an awful feeling that something terrible had happened, but quickly told himself not to be stupid. But he didn't altogether get rid of the queer feeling. It was like whistling in the dark cellar to stop yourself being scared, he thought. It always made you feel a bit better, but it didn't chase away *all* of the fear.

Trying to see the best side of things, he consoled himself that sometimes it was better being alone in the house with nobody else around. You had so much more freedom and could do practically anything you liked. You could even imagine you were a grown-up.

Sinking into the armchair his Dad always sat in, he thought, at least they left a lovely big fire on before they went out. His Mam must have banked it up as usual with the potato peelings and cinders. Roasting hot and glowing a beautiful deep orange colour, it reminded him of the big coke fires the Cocky Watchmen always had at night outside their huts, when the workmen would be mending or digging the roads up. And there was nothing more cosy and homely than a coke fire.

As he gazed around the kitchen with his feet up against the mantelpiece, he reckoned that their house was looking much more like a home these days. The smashed, boarded-up windows had all been replaced for Christmas, and for the first time he could remember, there wasn't a single pane broken out of the whole twelve. And the gas, which had been cut off for ages, was back on again. There was even a brand new gas mantle, which made the room and everything else much brighter. And to top it all, the wireless was working again, this time good and loud, without having to strain your ears to hear it. What made him feel really good about that, was being able now to learn all the words of great songs like *She Wears Red Feathers* and *Liberty Belle* and *Tennessee Waltz* and *Jezebel*.

He had Winston Sanders licked these days, he thought smugly, because not only could he talk about all the latest records on the wireless, he could also sing them, and take off people like Guy Mitchell and Frankie Laine and Johnnie Ray.

Children's Hour was still on and he was becoming desperately impatient for it to end. It was a stupid programme, he thought loftily. Having to suffer it reminded him of what his Dad had said about the wireless being all right for people who can't think for themselves - especially when you had to put up with stupid things like *Children's Hour*!

For the past few weeks, he had been following the adventures of *Curly Wee and Gussie Goose* in the *'Echo*, but his Mam or Dad weren't in to buy it. So, searching for lemonade bottles to take back to McDonough's, he finally found an empty Tizer bottle in the cupboard and dashed out and bought an *'Echo* with the twopence deposit on the bottle.

Back in the armchair, he felt truly grown-up, as he sat reading the newspaper with his feet again up against the mantelpiece. And like some Lord of the Manor, he was revelling so much in his own importance, and was so engrossed in pretending to be a grown-up that, despite the huge banner headline, the words weren't registering. When he did eventually focus on them, he was amazed to read, "The King Dies In His Sleep." But by the time he'd read the story the initial shock had subsided. All he could think of then was whether or not their school would get a day's holiday for the King's funeral. Anyway, he thought restlessly, fuck the King, I wonder where me Mam and Dad is?

It seemed that no sooner had *Dick Barton* started than it finished. It was always like that, he thought grudgingly. The good things are always over and finished with quickly, but the lousy things seem to go on for ever and ever. Still, he thought, *Ray's a Laugh* will be on soon, and later on *Variety Bandbox*, so there's still loads to look forward to. But he was still annoyed at having to wait, and couldn't understand why you always have to wait for the good things. Why can't everything, everywhere, be good all the time? Then everybody would be happy all the time. Surely, he thought, that wouldn't be so hard to do?

Apart from *Curly Wee and Gussie Goose*, and the King dying, there wasn't much in the paper of interest to him, apart from the usual news about Korea on page three, but even though Brendan was out there, he could never get interested enough to read about it. Probably, he thought, because he couldn't understand the strange names like *Syngman Rhee*, and places like *Pusan* and *Panmunjom* and *Seoul*. And because he could never fathom what things like the *38th Parallel* meant. He couldn't be bothered with things he didn't understand.

Throwing the newspaper to one side, he looked around for something to do. But, because his Mam had tidied up before she went out, the place was spotless, so he couldn't even pass the time cleaning up.

He hated February. It was light enough after school to tempt you out to play, but it was always so freezing cold, so that you couldn't go out. At least, he thought, in the proper winter you knew where you stood. October and November and December nights were always dark and cold quite early. But, just like the summer months, which were always light and warm, they didn't pretend to be anything else. There was something clear cut about them. They didn't want to be summer *and* winter, like February did. He began feeling there was something really sly about February. It reminded him of Winston Sanders: wanting the best of both worlds. Two-faced, he concluded. Yeah, that's what February was, two-faced.

Unable to resist the temptation any longer, he went over to the sideboard and, pretending to be Johnnie Ray, began singing to himself in the mirror. As he sang *Cry*, he imagined himself standing under the spotlight on stage in a vast theatre packed with people. He was putting everything he had into the sad love song, whilst silently telling himself how good he was and how much like Johnnie Ray he sounded. And, trying to make the impersonation as real as possible, he hunched his shoulders and made such dramatic gestures of anguish, that he actually looked broken-hearted himself.

When he'd finished the song, what surprised him more than anything else were the real tears on his cheeks. But instead of congratulating himself for giving such a realistic performance, he again felt the weird, scared feeling rising up inside. He knew why. He'd got too involved again. So, to halt the feeling in its tracks, he quickly wiped away the tears and, with a business-like sniff of his nose, smoothed down his jersey in order to get back to his normal self. It was good to know, he thought gratefully, that at times like this you could instantly get back to being your ordinary self, just by wiping your eyes and sniffing, and - even though it didn't need it - smoothing down the front of your jersey.

The man on the wireless was harping on about cows and pigs and farms. But never having been to the countryside, he wasn't in the least interested. In exasperation, he dashed over and violently switched it off. Then, after putting some coal on the fire, he worked his way back to the sideboard and the mirror.

Pulling the bottom drawer out, so that he could rest his foot on it, he leaned on his elbows and began smiling and frowning into the mirror. First, he smiled with his mouth closed, then open, showing his teeth. Next, he turned sideways, giving himself a sly sideward grin. Then turning full face again and trying to convey an amused, surprised expression, he raised his eyebrows so high that his forehead became wrinkled with long horizontal creases.

During the next hour he tried so many different expressions that his face felt exhausted, so he simply leaned there trying to stare himself out on the mirror. And as he continued to stare with deep concentration it seemed as if he had disappeared and there was now somebody else in his place. He couldn't recognise this strange person, but despite becoming more and more frightened, neither could he drag himself away.

It was a terrible feeling, like the nightmares he sometimes had, when he would be getting chased through the dark, rainy back streets by a murderer and his legs would feel numb and as heavy as lead, and no matter how much he tried, he couldn't run any faster, and the murderer was slowly catching up to him, until he finally grabbed him around the neck with his big strong hairy hands, and he would wake up petrified and covered in sweat. The sickening panic he now felt was exactly the same.

Eventually, he managed to twist his head sideways away from the mirror and break the horrifying spell. And, when he dared to look again, he was deeply thankful to see his own familiar face once again. It was deathly white and wore a really scared expression, but he thanked God it was still his own face. The sheer sense of relief dissolved most of the terror and made him feel much better, but the horrible parched and bitter taste of fear lingering in his mouth made him nauseous and sickly.

Desperate to get back to normality, he quickly put the kettle on and made himself a cup of tea. Then, switching the wireless back on, he sat down in the armchair, resting the cup on the tattered arm.

Radio Newsreel was now on and was all about the King's death, but he soon lost interest. And, as his mind wandered back to the mirror, it suddenly occurred to him that the face he always saw there, his own, would be with him till the day he died, and he'd never ever be able to shake it off or get rid of it. The mere idea of it weighed him down with a heavy feeling of being trapped. Anything else you got tired of, or fed up with, could be thrown away or changed or swapped for something else, he thought. Or, if it was your arm or your leg, you could even cut it off. But your face, your own face, the face that was the most familiar face in the world to you, you could never get rid of. It was so frightening to realise that, wherever you went and whatever you did, it would be with you all through your life. The fearful certainty that you were saddled with it for life and could never get rid of it, not even if you lived forever, seemed such a crushing burden. Yet, he thought in amazement, I've never actually seen it for *real*, and I never will. Come to that, he told himself, all that *anyone* has seen of their face is a reflection - and everyone knows everything is always back to front in the mirror.

The more he dwelt on it, the more its sheer inescapability filled him with dread and anxiety. This Thing, this Millstone, this Burden, this Face, he would have to carry all through his life: he didn't even know what it looked like. Not *really*.

Wouldn't it be lovely, he thought wistfully, if you could step outside of yourself, outside of your skin, whenever you wanted to, and take a look at your real self instead of just a reflection. Then, everybody would know what they looked like, not just to themselves, but to everyone else too. That would be really smashing if you could do that.

He felt suddenly proud of himself for thinking of such a good idea. And this good feeling seemed to drive away most of the gloom and dread and hopelessness. And to make things even better, *Ray's A Laugh* came on the wireless.

Chapter Eighteen

It was half-ten now and there was still no sign of his Mam and Dad. The uncomfortable feeling he'd had when he first came home from school hours earlier now returned. There's definitely something wrong, he thought ominously, I know there is, I can tell there is. And when he heard loud knocking at the front door and the sound of his Mam wailing, he knew he'd been right.

Dashing down the lobby, he quickly opened the front door and was surprised to see his Mam on the bottom step being propped up by Mr and Mrs Owens. She looked awful, all bedraggled like some rag doll.

Seeing his shocked expression, Mr Owens quietly said, "It's alright Sheridan, son. Can we come in a minute?"

They almost carried his wailing Mam along the lobby into the kitchen. Once in the gaslight, he saw that her hair was dishevelled and her eyes were red raw and bloodshot, as though she'd been crying for ages. Mr Owens was gently coaxing her to sit down and telling her in a kindly voice to have a cup of tea and that everything would be all right, when, without warning, she flung out her arms and let out an horrific scream, tearing wildly at her hair. And as the tears tore down her face, she howled in total despair, "Oh no! Oh no! Oh no! Oh Go...d no!"

Looking stupified at the Owens's, Sheridan was frightened out of his wits. He knew something horrible must have happened because, apart from the state his Mam was in, Mrs Owens, who had her arms around her, was on the verge of tears, and even Mr Owens wore a sombre expression. It was terrible not knowing what was going on.

"What's happened? What's me Mam crying for?" he asked frantically near to tears, but deep down not wanting to know, then adding anxiously, "Where's me Dad, Mr Owens?"

Without changing his expression, he said, "It's alright son. Yer mother's had some bad news, that's all. Everything'll be alright lad, don't worry."

Mrs Owens was stroking his Mam's hair, trying to soothe her, but his Mam couldn't seem to stop the heavy sobbing, which was now convulsing her whole body. Suddenly, she started howling again like a madwoman.

"Oh, my poor Brendan!" she shrieked. "My beautiful son! My beautiful son! My poor lad! My angel! He never harmed a soul in his life! Oh God! What am I gonna do!"

Hearing this, the impact hit Sheridan in the belly with the force of a sledgehammer, making him dizzy and sick as the panic and confusion assailed him from all sides. Everything inside of him seemed to be jumping and jerking madly out of control. Every nerve in his body felt on fire, making him shake uncontrollably. But strangely, no tears came. It was too early yet.

Still reeling under the terrible force of the impact, he sensed, he KNEW, that what had happened was the very worst thing in the world - Brendan was dead!

He heard Mr Owens's quiet voice, as if a million miles away, urgently telling his wife to put the kettle on and make a pot of tea, then gently telling his Mam to bear up and that time was a great healer. But although everything seemed so far away and unreal, he was determined to fight back and not to be overwhelmed by it all. Somebody had to stick up for the family. What would the Owens's think of their family, he thought, all crying their bleedin' eyes out like babies and making a show of themselves?

Taking the cup of tea from Mrs Owens, he took a few quick gulps, and although it burned his throat, it seemed to clear his head slightly, so that he was able to pull himself together. But he still couldn't stop the tears from welling up.

"Where's me Dad, Mr Owens?" he again asked, but this time more calmly, not begging like before.

He was forcing himself to be brave and act like a man, so that he would be treated with respect and told everything. And Mr Owens seemed to understand and respect him for trying to be so brave and grown-up.

"I'm sorry lad", he said, "but yer Dad's been pinched. We met yer mother on the corner crying her eyes out. She's drunk, so we brought her down home."

"But what's he been pinched for?" he pleaded.

His Mam seemed to be in a world of her own, her body still shaking with the heavy sobbing, as Mrs Owens said to her husband, "Eh Bob, I think they'll have to stay in our house tonight. We can't leave them here on their own."

Nodding his agreement, he then turned to Sheridan and, in an attempt to restore some normality, said lightly "Would yer like to sleep with our Freddy for tonight son? You'se two get on well with each other don't yiz?"

He couldn't answer immediately, because of a choking lump in his throat. Then suddenly the tears that had been welling up poured out in a torrent. He had tried his best to stem them, but couldn't hold back any longer. Running over to his Mam, he grabbed her around her neck with both arms and hugged her as hard as he could. Raising her head, she clung to him tightly and smothered him with kisses, their boiling hot tears mingling until their faces were soaking wet.

"Poor Brendan, son", she groaned with utter despair, "Poor Brendan's been killed. Oh God, what am I gonna do?"

She seemed to him like a little, innocent, helpless child, as she caught her breath amid the sobs and sighed heavily, "Oh, God help me!"

To distract himself from this incredible situation, he tried to concentrate on ordinary everyday things, and even forced himself amid the tears to sound normal. "Well, I suppose I've had me Scholarship now."

But nobody answered.

Hoping Mrs Owens would be more forthcoming than her husband, he again asked, "What's me Dad been pinched for?"

But she merely glanced cautiously at her husband as if to say, "Shall I tell him?"

But she need not have worried. Turning to Sheridan with a determined expression, he said, "Well according to yer Mam, yer Dad went down to Chinatown and smashed all the windows in the cafes to get his own back on them for Brendan."

Then, in a gentler tone, he quickly added, "But don't worry son, we'll go down the court first thing in the morning to see if we can get him bail. He'll probably be home tomorrow, so don't you worry yerself."

A new wave of tears erupted and spilled down his face. It seemed to him that the only way to get any relief from this overpowering nightmare was to have your eyes refilled every few minutes with fresh tears, even though you had to keep wiping them away with your sleeve in order to see properly.

"Are yer sure, Mr Owens?" he cried, desperately searching for the smallest sign of comfort, "Honest, will he be able to come home tomorrow?"

Trying to appear confident, he said, "Honest to God, son. You just try and not to worry."

Clutching at any shred of hope, he sobbed, "Ah eh Mr Owens, it's not true about our Brendan is it? He's not really dead, is he?" It seemed impossible to take in. He was hoping with all his might that it was a lie or a mistake, or that he was just having a nightmare, and that his Mam was only in that state through missing Brendan, who was so far away from home. Or simply because she was drunk. After all, he thought, she *was* always talking about Brendan and how much she missed him, and she *did* more or less always cry when she was drunk, didn't she?

But when Mr Owens spoke again, his hopes were finally dashed and he felt himself being pushed back down into the darkness and the pain and the hopelessness.

"I'm sorry, lad", he replied with ruthless certainty, "but it's the truth. He *is* dead. He's been killed in action. Yer Mam showed us the telegram she got this afternoon."

At that moment, he hated Mr Owens for robbing him of his last glimmer of hope, leaving him without any relief from this devastating horror. And, although he continued talking to him sympathetically, his words were just a meaningless jumble to Sheridan.

His Mam was now howling again in a low animal-like wail.

"I want my Brendan... my poor lovely Brendan... I want my lad... my lovely boy!"

Seeing her soaking wet bloodshot eyes rolling round and round, Sheridan became even more terrified, for she seemed to be going out of her mind. Mrs Owens was doing her best to soothe her, but it was no good. So she began helping her out of the armchair.

"Come on, Katy", she was murmuring softly. "Come on love, you're coming with us, everything's gonna be alright. You'll see."

But as she gently helped her along the lobby, his distraught Mam seemed a million miles away.

Putting a strong arm around Sheridan, Mr Owens said with forced casualness, "Come on Sheridan, are yer coming? We're all going to our house for tonight. Come on son, try and put it out of yer mind. Yer Dad'll be out tomorrow, and your Thomas'll be home in a couple of days."

Following them down the lobby, the mention of his Dad and Thomas buoyed him up slightly, and helped him to try and act as normal as possible.

"Is your Freddy in bed?" he asked lightly. But he didn't feel in the slightest normal. He knew he was only whistling in the dark again, like he did with the snails in the cellar. But Mr Owens, who was also pretending to sound lighthearted, replied, "Hope he is, cheeky little bleeder. Smack his friggin' arse if he isn't."

Doing his best to appear interested, he said, "Yer know what Mr Owens, he told us he always stays up late, and never goes to bed before twelve o'clock."

But he was talking mechanically, for its own sake, to keep his mind from wandering back to the heavy fog of confusion and shock and grief. In truth, he couldn't care a damn right now whether Freddy was in bed or not.

In the Owens's they gave his Mam another cup of tea, but Sheridan refused any more, because he felt so sickly. Mrs Owens also gave his Mam two big white tablets and told her they would make her sleep. And after swallowing them, she eventually seemed to quieten down. But as they were easing her into an armchair by the fire, she still couldn't stop sobbing.

When they had arrived at the Owens's, the kitchen was empty except for the new baby, fast asleep in a makeshift cot in a bottom drawer of the sideboard and Freddy *was* in bed after all.

After attending to the baby, Mrs Owens said with a studious expression, "Tell yer what Bob, on second thoughts, we'll let Freddy sleep with us and let Katy and Sheridan go in his bed, eh?"

"Yeah okay, Queen", he replied.

As they were talking, his Mam, who had put the cup of tea on the hearth untouched, was silent now except for the quiet sobbing and sniffling as she tried to clear her nose. He could hardly bear to look at her. It seemed to him that she would always be crying now for the rest of her life.

Later, when he was cuddled up to her in bed in the darkness, he too began to quietly cry, and the pain and sorrow didn't seem so bad. But he was glad when she eventually drifted off to sleep. He couldn't sleep though, as he fought to keep his mind off Brendan and what had happened. Adrift in the thick maze of shock and sorrow, his thoughts and feelings were at once so confused and chaotic, making him feel anxious and guilty and stupid.

He wouldn't be going to school tomorrow. That's for sure, he thought. Not after this. The prospect of sitting the Scholarship, which he'd been looking forward to for weeks, was now completely out of the question. Anyway, he thought, I probably wouldn't have stood a dog's chance of passing anyhow.

As the night wore on and his Mam began snoring, he tried and tried to fall asleep, but the more he tried, the more awake he became. But it had nothing to do with his Mam's snoring. It was his mind that wouldn't let him sleep. It was crowded with countless thoughts and images that hopped, skipped and jumped from one to the other, every one seeming to be saturated with the flavour and heavy atmosphere of intense sadness. But every time any of these thoughts tempted him to wander actually back to Brendan, he'd quickly draw back, like you would from the edge of a precipice.

He simply couldn't take it in that his big brother was dead. It was so utterly unbelievable. It was like when Sloppy Joe Flaherty got killed - only a million times worse. And to think, that like Flaherty, he'd never see Brendan again for as long as he lived, even if he lived to be a hundred! But this time, it was his big brother! Oh no! It couldn't be! Things like that didn't happen to their family. It wasn't real. Not their Brendan. It was too horrific. It was too painful, it just wasn't *believable*. You couldn't accept things like that. And he knew that he never would. But he still knew deep, deep down that there was no escape from the brutal truth - Brendan was *dead*. It was like being cut off in a back entry facing a huge brick wall that blocked you from the only way out, and from *ever* getting out!

Later, long into the dark night, when everything was deathly silent, save for his Mam's heavy cluttered breathing, he at last began to feel more relaxed. But sleep still would not come. And as he drew comfort from cuddling even closer to his Mam, he realised that pretty soon he wouldn't even be able to do that without being called a "mammy's lad". It seemed that the older you got, the less you had to look forward to. Even now, it seemed to him that there would never again be anything to look forward to. And even if there were, it would be so petty and meaningless compared to losing Brendan, that it wouldn't even be worth looking forward to.

Somehow, he didn't feel like a kid anymore. He didn't even feel the same as when he'd come home from school yesterday. His childhood seemed to have vanished in one single day. He'd always longed to be grown-up, but he'd also noticed that, when you got what you'd always wanted, you didn't want it anymore. He'd noticed that with lots of things, and it made him absolutely certain he'd never be happy again. He'd always more or less been unhappy, and now he was still unhappy - but a million times more so. Strangely, he seemed resigned to this sort of "inbuilt" unhappiness now. Deep down, in the far off "third eye" audience part of him, it seemed there had always been something nagging at him, like an omen or demon's voice, begrudging him any happiness and making him feel guilty whenever he was happy. Even when he'd sometimes felt slightly happy, free from the nervousness and dread of the drunken Saturday nights, it had always been there in the background, nagging and threatening him that one day he would have to pay some kind of price.

Now he knew what the price was. Now this omen or demon's voice or fate or whatever it was, had finally punished him more severely than he'd ever expected, and he hated it with all of his being. There was no need for it to kill Brendan, he thought. It could have punished him in a million ways without killing Brendan. It was as unfair as getting six strokes of Black Bess across your arse, just for being late. It was out of all proportion.

And the fucking, poxy, disgusting omen or demon or fate, or whatever it was, was a fucking hateful bastard!

He had never bothered to question exactly why he'd always felt so guilty and why he'd simply taken it for granted that he would one day be punished, why he'd always regarded it as inevitable. He just did. He didn't even know what he was guilty of, but he strongly suspected it had something to do with him playing with himself, even after his Dad had warned him about it. But then, he thought, it couldn't only be that. He'd always had this feeling for as long as he could remember, even before he'd ever started doing it.

As his mind slipped back to Brendan, he was suddenly hit with a most powerful blow in his stomach and the terrible thought that, if only he had warned him that night about the men in the black car, poor Brendan would be alive now. It was altogether too much for him. A new wave of despair engulfed him as he tried not to waken his Mam with his sobbing.

When sleep came and finally released him from his torment, he fell into the most beautiful dream of his whole life.

He was back in the house, and Thomas was home and his Mam and Dad were sober, and there was a big roaring fire on in the fireplace, and everyone was happy. And he was staring into the large mirror of the massive Victorian ebony sideboard. Only this time he was a very important person for staring into the mirror. For what reason he didn't know. It was just like being the only one in the family able to play the piano - everyone respected and admired you.

As he focused, harder and harder into the mirror, he gradually saw his Mam's and Dad's and Thomas's faces appear behind him, and they were smiling and full of pride. Then other faces began to appear: Mr Henry's and Mr Wilkes's and Mr Usher's.

Then Mrs Dodson's, the Headmistress from the Infants and even Waxen Face Miss Jones's. Then Flaherty's face came into focus, amid those of Mr and Mrs Owens's. Then Freddy's, then Reggie's. And all of them were happy and laughing and smiling. And the harder he stared, his own face, in the centre of the mirror, slowly began to change into somebody else's. But this time he didn't become panicky or scared like he'd always done in the past, because he could see, and they could all see, that the face it was changing into was none other than Brendan's!

Brendan's face, which at first wore a broad smile, now blossomed out into full blown laughter. And as it laughed and laughed and laughed, he looked the happiest person in the world. Sheridan then heard the sound of thousands of people cheering and clapping all around him, and a woman's heavenly voice, full of awe, echoing through the crowds so that everybody could hear.

"Oh, what a beautiful gift he's got!" she sighed. She was talking about him, and all the applause was for him. God! For the first time in his life he felt important. Nobody was looking down on him anymore. Instead, people were looking up to him. He was *special*. No more feeling wretched for being poor. No more of the terrible oppressive guilt. No more stigma. He had power. He was famous! He was SOMEONE!

And that was because any time anyone wanted to see Brendan, they only had to come to the mirror with him. And the most wonderful part was that, every time he did it, he was killing two birds with one stone. Because each time Brendan's face appeared, he could get rid of the most familiar face in the world - his own. And nobody, nobody in the whole wide world could do *that*.

Also By The Author

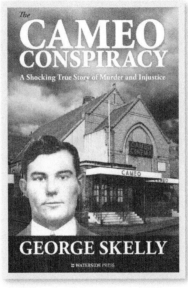